IN PRAISE OF
HOPE FOR FAMILIES IN RECOVERY

Mark and Janet have done an exceptional job addressing the issue of substance abuse, by educating both the individual, the family, and those assisting them. They have taken a very complex topic and have broken it down and discussed it in a manner that's easy to understand for individuals, families, and all those helping. Above all, they have stayed true to the title of their book by giving "hope for families in recovery and helping them find their way back home." This book is a true gift of hope to all families in search of it.

MONICA FERKIN, ACSW, LCSW, CADC

As a radiologist who has practiced for more than 34 years, I see the profound negative health effects of addiction on a daily basis: falls, motor vehicle accidents, acute and chronic internal organ injury and, of course, devastating permanent brain injuries, to name a few. The guidelines in this book help to identify root causes of addiction so that a treatment approach can be implemented and, most importantly, create an environment to prevent addiction from occurring in the first place. I believe this book is a must-read for virtually everyone. It is extremely well written—complete yet concise. It should be part of our education system and may stem some of the root causes of addiction at an age when people are most vulnerable and easily influenced. Reading the Constitution is required in middle school. How can you pursue life, liberty and happiness if you have an addiction?

GREG ZWEIG, MD

Mark and Janet Myers have over 30 years of experience dealing with substance use disorders (SUD), and they address them comprehensively. If you're looking for an all-encompassing guide on how to attack, cope with, and overcome any form of SUD, this book has it. As an expert in dealing with change, I can attest that they address head-on the fear of change, hopelessness, and how to create a desire for the user to change. What I love about this book is that it provides the family with a roadmap for handling the emotions of stress, anger, feelings of betrayal, guilt, and uncertainty associated with substance use disorders. It's not just the substance user who is affected; the entire family has to deal with this problem, and Mark and Janet will walk you through each step of this journey. I highly recommend you let these experts show you how to win this war on addiction.

ROBERT STEVENSON, Global Keynote Speaker,
Best-Selling Author and Consultant

This profound exploration shifts the focus from stigmatizing terms to understanding the nuanced struggles and resilience of families navigating the turbulent path of recovery. It delves into the emotional upheavals and triumphs that define the family experience, offering a compassionate roadmap for healing and reconnection. A thorough, well-rounded read that covers the entire path of recovery from impact on family to triggers, from building trust to relapses, all the way to treatment options and support systems, a very thorough guide!

STEPHANIE KROLL

Mark and Janet's book offers a vital roadmap for navigating the complexities of substance abuse. With empathy and expertise, the authors illuminate the often-overlooked perspectives of families grappling with addiction. Their clear and accessible writing style makes complex issues understandable, providing practical guidance on recognizing warning signs, fostering motivation for change, and managing triggers. This book is an invaluable resource for anyone affected by substance use disorder and promises to be a trusted companion on the path to recovery.

DAN BLAIR, LMFT, LCPC, NCPC, CAMS, Blair Counseling and Mediation

This book is very informative about the addiction process. Addiction is a complicated disease. Mark and Janet did a wonderful job covering all aspects, including the family illness, making the reading understandable for all.

SCOTT WAHLER, Retired CAD

This book is a masterful, easy to read explanation of how families can recover from the terrible effects of a substance abusing member. It makes it easy for a family member or substance users to understand and identify the obstacles that prevent recovery. The compassionate, easy to understand explanations of science and techniques for recovery readily inspires the reader to take the next step. This is a must-read for anyone who wants to involve their closest support persons in recovery.

KAREN LYNN CASSIDAY, PhD, ACT, Owner and Managing Director, Anxiety Treatment Center of Greater Chicago

Hope For Families in Recovery

Finding Our Way Home

Mark Myers, LCSW, CADC

Janet Myers, LCSW

Hope For Families in Recovery: Finding Our Way Home

Mark & Janet Myers

ISBN-13: 979-8-218-50119-8
Library of Congress Control Number: 2024918023

Falling Trees Publication
Crystal Lake, Illinois
mark@myerscounseling.com
janet@myerscounseling.com

This book is manufactured in the United States of America.

Editor: Janet Schwind
Graphic Designer: Suzanne Parada
Illustrator: Angelina Palladini
Photographer: Layla Tichy

CONTENTS

Foreword

I was the last person on earth who thought anyone would ever ask to write a foreword for their book. You see, I have known Janet my entire life, as she is my sister and Mark is my brother-in-law for the last 30 years. Janet and Mark met when they bonded over their passion for helping others working in a residential treatment center and built Myers Counseling Group together, which has been in business for 25 years.

Mark has been a Licensed Clinical Social Worker and Certified Alcohol and Drug Counselor since before they met, and Janet is a Licensed Clinical Social Worker. Both have extensive experience working with adults, teens, and families with mental health and substance use disorders. Another aspect of their intimate knowledge of substance use disorder is that Janet and I grew up in a family with substance use disorder. Our father and his parents suffered with alcoholism and he eventually recovered. Our youngest brother lost his battle with the bottle after many years of struggle. I am a recovering alcoholic with less than 2 years of sobriety under my belt. As a family, we are breaking the cycle of substance use disorder. *Hope for Families in Recovery: Finding Our Way Home* addresses how families can heal and what roles each person will play in the recovery process. Substance use does not have to be the "dirty" family secret or as they write in the book the "silent agreement."

Although "home is where the heart is," it may look very different as you go through the recovery process. So much has to change and you will not be left the same, but that's okay! I encourage you to read *Hope for Families in Recovery* and share it with your family or support system because healing is possible.

Karen Rae

Introduction

"Every day is a journey, and the journey itself is home."

~Basho

What do we call the collection of experiences that happen around alcohol, drugs, or addictive behaviors? Alcoholism. Addiction. Alcohol problem. Alcohol use disorder. Drug problem. Problem user. Problem drinker. Substance abuse problem. It is pivotal to identify what happens in the lives of users and family members in a way that doesn't label the individual.

Considerable discussion has occurred in the mental health profession around what to name these disorders, and its approach regarding these problems has changed significantly over the years. Our knowledge about the human body and brain continues to be added to our toolbox. Pharmaceutical discoveries aid in our fight against substance use and mental health problems. Even the way we define substance abuse has changed. In 2013, the mental health field altered the way we describe people who have challenges with drugs or alcohol. Instead of addiction, we now use the term substance use disorder (SUD).

Labeling creates barriers to treatment that prevent the individual from seeking help. At the same time, we don't want to minimize the seriousness of these disorders and the impact they have on the lives of individuals and families. As such, in this book we will use the phrase "a person with substance use disorder (SUD)" to refer to someone who struggles with substances, as opposed to the terms "alcoholic" or "addict." At times, we may refer to addiction or abuse to describe the disorder and will use these interchangeably, as well.

Our first book, *Falling Trees, Color Blind Scientists, & Addiction*, discussed the complexities of addressing a substance use problem from the perspective of the user (1). A substance use disorder looks different depending on the lens with which you view it. Although we discussed families in our first book, we decided there was much more to cover. In *Hope for Families in Recovery: Finding our Way Home*, we expand on how SUD impacts the family.

"Family" means something different to everyone. The family you're born into may not be the family that meets your needs. Our book uses the word family to identify the people who populate your life and give you the sense of belonging a biological family should. Your version of family may be ever-changing throughout your lifespan and circumstances. So, we invite you to envision family as you define it for yourself. For us, family currently looks like just Mark, Janet, and a houseful of pets; our three children are grown and living their own lives. For others, it may be living alone, or you may live with a partner or friends who you consider family. You may live in a family that's traditional or non-traditional. Maybe you reject your family of origin. There are people who create their own families and support systems.

Home refers to the place life comes together for you. It may not be a physical place, but an emotional one. A place of safety and connection. It may be a space you occupy with people in your life, or it may be a feeling you have about the place you inhabit with people you love. Again, we invite you to define what home looks like for you.

Every family's journey is unique. The definition of home may change significantly for all family members throughout recovery as we learn to create a safe place for all involved. In *Hope for Families in Recovery*, we focus primarily on the family. They are survivors of the disorder as well. The impact for them as they attempt to find answers and rebuild their lives requires commitment and tenacity. We hope you find help for your journey as we forge a new way home.

Home may not be the same as it was before the substance use disorder. The outcomes vary because families must create a new normal. There is rebuilding relationships, developing trust, working past triggers, and establishing new and different relationships inside and outside the family. For the user, they reconnect with their family and find their place in the family system. Finding your home means getting to where you feel centered or connected despite all that has happened. The impact of SUD takes families in all different directions. Being home is not a physical spot but an emotional one. It means the journey continues with an evolving perspective on home. Recovery from SUD is a lifetime process, not an event. Families can find peace and happiness with or without the user's abstinence. Emotional scars do heal in time. Family members can find their own way home regardless of the decisions the substance user makes. Our book offers hope, healing, and direction through the process of recovery.

It's a challenging road for families to navigate. Stopping the use, regardless of the drug of choice, does not magically make everything better. Early recovery is stressful for families. All involved face obstacles, including adapting roles, developing trust, and moving past resentments. Family recovery involves finding direction, hope, connection, and resources to overcome the difficulties created by SUD. Calling upon our 30 years' devotion to helping families recover and rebuild, *Hope for Families in Recovery* addresses the multiple impacts substance problems have on the family and how to navigate this recovery journey with hope. It provides a clear pathway out of the weeds and into a new life of peace, healing and connection. We pray you find your way to a home filled with safety and connection.

Mark and Janet Myers

CHAPTER 1

Defining Substance Use Disorder

**"When substance use progresses to the point of addiction,
a person no longer chooses to use drugs or alcohol;
they are compelled despite the consequences."**

~Mark and Janet Myers

Substance use disorder is a mental health condition that exists on a spectrum from mild and moderate to severe. An SUD occurs when an unhealthy pattern of alcohol or drug use interferes with the life and functioning of the user. When substance use progresses to the point of addiction, a person no longer chooses to use drugs or alcohol; they are compelled despite the consequences. They depend on substances to relax, feel normal, or enjoy life. A key sign of addiction is a loss of control over substance use. Loss of control refers to being unable to set and maintain limits on one's use.

The *Diagnostic and Statistical Manual 5-R* identifies eleven criteria for substance use disorder, used in the mental health field to render diagnoses (2). Diagnosis is helpful in the treatment of SUD and mental health disorders because it allows us to develop a common language around the challenges involved in understanding the impact of the disorder, as well as the treatment of such a condition. If an individual has two to three of the eleven, they have a mild disorder. Four to five identify a moderate disorder, and six or more diagnose a severe disorder. The criteria include:

1. **Increasing tolerance to substances** or needing more of the substance to achieve the same effects.

2. **Withdrawal symptoms** - When not using, there are significant physical and emotional signs (i.e., trouble sleeping, nausea/vomiting, diarrhea, sweating, shaking, tiredness, moodiness, cravings, depression, anxiety, etc.)

3. Engaging in **dangerous behavior** when using (i.e., driving, fighting, risky settings, etc.)

4. Use causes **relationship problems.**

5. **Neglecting responsibilities** at work, home, or school because of use

6. **Using more significant amounts** of the substance over an extended period

7. **Repeated unsuccessful attempts** to cut down or stop use

8. Experience intense **cravings or urges** to use

9. **Using substances instead** of engaging in social and recreational activities

10. Spending **more time acquiring, using, and recovering** from substance use

11. **Continuing to use despite consequences** to physical and mental health

Spectrum of Use

Specific characteristics put individuals at higher risk of experiencing the effects of SUD. We call these **risk factors**. These make an individual more likely to develop the disease of substance use. They fall into three levels: biological, psychological, and social. For example, a genetic predisposition to becoming addicted to substances or strong environmental influences to use substances would be classified as a biological risk factor.

Protective factors are the circumstances that prevent or reduce the likelihood of developing substance use disorder. Many of the protective factors reduce the impact of risks and create resilience in individuals or families. Examples include: a positive relationship with parents or delayed onset of substance use. They also fall into three levels: biological, psychological, and social. Some risk and protective factors do not change much over time and are considered fixed. Others can vary throughout our lifetime.

The interaction of the various risk and protective factors (see chart) creates unique challenges for each user and those who love them. There are multiple points of view on addiction, that of the substance user and family. Each family member has their journey through recovery. We cannot change some risk factors, but protective factors can mitigate potential damage.

Protective Factors

- Positive Outlook
- Supportive family/home environment
- Being involved in school activities (youth)
- Strong social connections (church, community, school)
- Supportive peer group with strong moral compus
- Strong sense of confidence
- Good coping and problem solving skills
- Safe environment

> Protective factors can be environmental, psychological, or historical events, situations, or traits. They decrease the likelihood of individuals developing a SUD.

VS

Risk Factors

- History/current of sexual, physical, or emotional abuse.
- Concurrent mental Health issue
- Low self esteem
- Disconnected from family
- Parents who use drugs (youth)
- Exposure to drugs/alcohol
- Lack of supervison (youth)
- Low stress tolerance.
- A peer group that supports heavy use.

> Risk factors can be environmental, psychological, or historical events, situations, or traits. They increase the likelihood of individuals developing a SUD.

Like diabetes, cancer, and heart disease, addiction develops from a combination of circumstances. These include behavioral, psychological, environmental, and biological factors. The genes passed on by parents play a crucial role. About half of a person's risk of developing a substance use disorder is genetic. When untreated, other physical and mental health issues evolve. Over time, SUD can become severe, disabling, and life-threatening. We may be unable to mitigate the risks, but we can limit them with protective factors.

There are no easy answers or quick fixes. Substance use problems develop over time. Financial, emotional, and physical pain have far-reaching consequences. The longer the use goes on, the more damage occurs. Some impact of the use can last a lifetime. Management of SUD in a family unit requires changes in strategies and perspectives to learn to navigate their way to a healthier place.

Different Perspectives

Families all experience and address SUD in diverse ways. When we use the term addict or addiction, some may have a stereotypical picture in mind of someone who uses alcohol or drugs. However, substance use has a wide reach and affects people from all walks of life. There are high-functioning addicts that somehow manage to avoid the negative consequences associated with regular use. Substance use affects many individuals including a teacher, lawyer, doctor, insurance agent, or stay-at-home mom. It will not look as one may expect. Often, our **perceptions** of addiction present a roadblock for both the family and the user. It makes it challenging to identify substance use as a problem. They simply do not see their loved one fitting into how they view a substance abuser. Families and users must understand that the signs can be subtle, but the impact is enormous.

Ideally, in the family, roles and responsibilities are shared, and they find balance. Substance use throws off that equilibrium. To regain stability, families adjust. When one part of the family breaks down, other parts must fill the gap. Maintaining balance is necessary for families to function as a unit. When the breakdown happens in the SUD family, it creates conflict and dysfunction. Stress, changing family roles, crossed or loosely defined boundaries, and financial, emotional, and social problems occur. Emotions such as shame, anger, feelings of betrayal, confusion, guilt, and uncertainty are everyday struggles they face.

The perceptions of family members regarding substance use can sometimes be inaccurate, colored by the lens with which the user is viewed. One common way of looking at substance use disorder is seeing it as a bad habit. On the one hand, categorizing SUD with other less harmful habits such as nail biting, leaving your dirty socks on the floor, and not cleaning up after yourself minimizes the impact of the problem. It also leads to shame on the user's part if they cannot stop their use. SUD goes well beyond habit and is accompanied by neurological, psychological, and physical implications. There are habit forming aspects that must be taken into consideration, but it is a significantly more complex issue than that.

Emotional issues for the user and family can be intense and complicated. Acknowledging a problem is difficult for families. Sometimes, the user or part of the family avoids talking about or acknowledging the issue. The silence impacts other family members who want to address their concerns. Their confidence in their own perceptions or sense of normalcy is shaken. They doubt their conclusions or observations.

In this book, we will help SUD families navigate through the experiences of broken promises, raised and dashed hope, denial, upheaval, and uncertainty. It is a formidable road for families to navigate. Stopping the use, whatever the drug of choice, does not magically make everything better. Sometimes, it is more stressful to have a sober family member in early recovery. The challenges of managing their recovery and building back trust within the family can be demanding. As we progress through the stages together, we will provide you with direction and insight into SUD, making this journey easier. Remember that these are not linear stages that progress in a particular order. Some may progress quickly, and others more slowly.

Stages of Recovery for Families: What to Expect

Recovery for both the user and the family follows an unpredictable path. A user's experience will impact the family, and the family's experience will influence the user. This interplay is tricky and makes the course of treatment and outcomes unique for every family. Substance use disorder affects all aspects of family life. SUD progression disrupts lives, and families lose connection, hope, and identity. The process of changing and reversing the damage caused by substance abuse is painful and difficult, resulting in an unknown path. The individual with SUD does not always successfully manage and recover from the disorder. Still, the family can heal and overcome the results of SUD even if the user continues to abuse substances.

Stage One: Avoidance

During this stage, the user actively abuses substances. Though aware of regular use, family members may not identify it as problematic. The hallmark of this stage is denial on the part of the user as well as the family. As the user's behavior impacts others, families accommodate the use and the consequences of SUD. Families are fearful of addressing the use or its impact. There is an active investment to resist addressing the issue. Families are not open to discussing substance use as a problem. Some reactions to the problem include denial, defensiveness, dismissal, and avoidance.

Stage Two: Awareness

In this stage, the families begin to talk about what they see. They acknowledge a potential problem and still need to address the issue entirely. There needs to be a consistent action plan. The family spends more time discussing the use. They have not fully accepted the use is a problem they must address.

There is some frustration and anger from family members. However, the family needs to focus on a plan of action or on directly managing the use. There may be some vague commitments from the abuser, such as "I will cut back" or "I will slow down" but not definitive action plans or commitments. The user may slow or reduce their use. The family speaks more openly about the problem and more consistently identifies the issue as a problem but tends to minimize and compensate for the shortcomings of the substance user. In contrast, the user minimizes the seriousness of the issue.

Stage 3: Action

Families talk more openly about the use and its impact on them. There is a consistent dialogue about substance abuse. The family has experienced broken promises, avoidance, and consequences for the use. The user can no longer avoid the topic. The family asks for a commitment to stop or consistently moderate the use. **Two paths** evolve from this stage. The first direction is dictated by the user's decisions. The second is directed by the family.

The *first path* is **directed by the user's response** and occurs if the user commits to abstaining or moderating their use. They develop a specific plan of action. At this point, treatment or outside support becomes an integral part of the journey. There are several levels of treatment available based on the needs of the individual. Those will be covered in later chapters.

The tasks of the family become more complicated during this stage as well. Adjusting their lifestyle to support the individual in recovery leads to complex decisions for each family member. Both the user and family member must address mental health issues that arise. Frequently, once substance use stops, other problems present themselves. The substance was being used to mask the symptoms of a mental health issue or family issue. Once the substance is removed, the problems resurface in a more overt manner.

Recovery tends to expose wounds within the family that need to be identified, including spousal or family attitudes toward substances, marital concerns, or mental health issues within the family. Acceptance is a significant step in this stage. The user accepts they engage in problematic behavior and cannot take control of the use without help. The family accepts that a significant problem exists that takes effort to resolve but disapproves of the behavior. This distinction is important because setting limits and helping the individual understand the consequences of not changing their use will impact the relationship.

The *second path* is directed by **a decision from the family** as a unit. The second path splits off into three directions: change, adjust, or leave.

1. They can *change* by getting help for themselves, even if the substance user does not accept help. Making changes within the family that offer the user the option to change while acquiring their own help can be a pivotal recovery decision for families.

2. Another option the family has is to *adjust*. They can continue to stay in the situation without making significant changes for themselves and accept that the substance user has decided not to make any changes. They work on coping with the substance user's behavior and choose not to have conflict over it.

3. Finally, they can *leave* the situation, and many partners/family members do leave during this time, or they separate for the period that the user continues to engage in substance abuse.

Stage 4: Adapting

In this stage, the user commits to abstain from substance use or actively moderates their use. The family and user decide to eliminate the problem and work together to repair the relationship. The challenges of Stage 4 include fixing the damage to relationships and family roles that occurred during active use. While the family may be opening itself to healing, there has been trauma to relationships and the individuals that make up the family. Each must find a way to heal and adapt to the changes within the family. Therapy and consistent effort to make changes are necessary. Although there are no guarantees at this stage for either the family or the user, many families successfully heal from SUD. The focus for this stage of treatment is to find a way to trust one another, build, and repair.

Beyond the stages

Sometimes, the consequences accumulated from the use may create too much impact, and repair seems improbable. Despite their best efforts, the user may need help to maintain the agreed-upon goal successfully. The long-term physical, mental, emotional, and relational consequences of continuing to use do cause some individuals and families to be overwhelmed. Although there is no guarantee that the outcomes will be what we hope, families who fully invest in recovery for themselves can heal. Home may be fundamentally changed.

Notes for the Journey Home

Substance use is a mental health disorder that affects users and the people who love them. SUDs occur on a spectrum from mild to severe. Even a mild disorder can disrupt lives and relationships, depending on the decision that the user makes. Understanding the perspectives of family and others aids in decision making and help to determine direction.

4 STAGES OF SUBSTANCE USE RECOVERYFOR FAMILIES

STAGE ONE - AVOIDANCE

In this stage, the user does not identify there is a problem and the family is unwilling, unable, or unaware of the impact of the use for the user and one another.

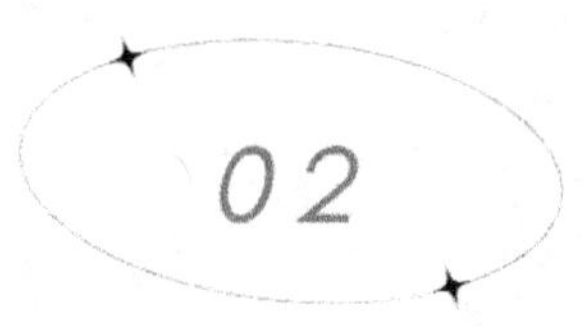

STAGE TWO - AWARENESS

Use continues and families begin to see begin to as problematic. They may Point out the use. The user may temporarily cut back, but there is not clear commitment to do so. The family acknowledges problem among themselves.

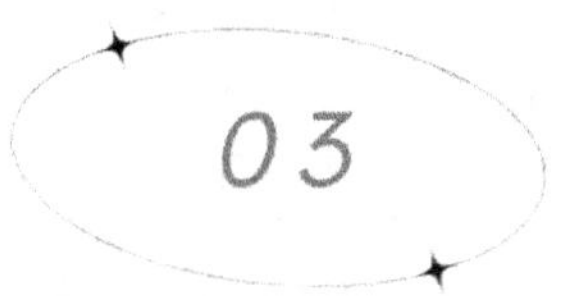

STAGE THREE - ACTION

The user can't avoid the Topic of their use. The Family sets limits. Commitments are made and broken.

The user commits to abstaining or moderating use. They commit to a specific plan of action including plans for slips and relapse prevention. The family is committed to supporting the user's sobriety Plan. This may not be a Straight path. Accountability measures and treatment are important aspects of this option.

The family sets limits and the user can't or won't agree or maintain the plan proposed by the family

Change
The Family member stays in the situation but chooses to receive treatment and support while the user continues to progress

Adjust
Family stays in the situation but tolerates the use without support or treatment

Leave
Family members choose to move out of the situation

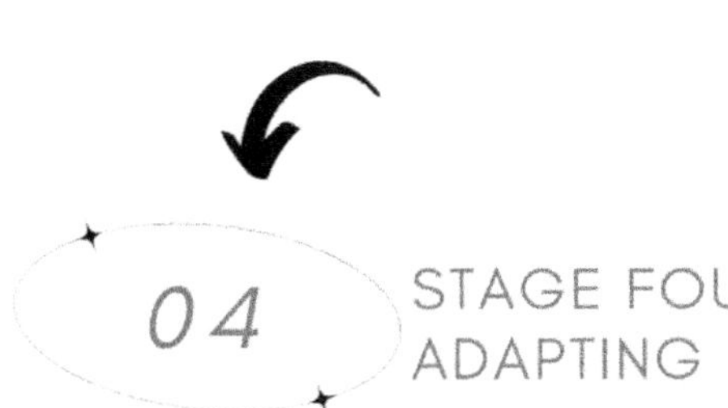

STAGE FOUR ADAPTING

In this stage, the user is committed to abstaining from using or moderating their use. The family and user are committed to eliminating the problem and working together to repair the relationship. The family is opening itself to healing.

$$\cdot\ \cdot\ \cdot\ \cdot\ \cdot\ \cdot$$

CHAPTER 2

Impact on the Substance User

$$\cdot\ \cdot\ \cdot\ \cdot\ \cdot\ \cdot$$

**"In describing the hurdles users face, we are not giving the person
a free pass for their misuse. We are only pointing out how difficult
it can be for users to stop. SUD is a self-feeding disease."**

~Mark and Janet Myers

The average person may not understand how or why somebody would put themselves through the consequences of substance use disorder. Common sense should tell them to stop. Why would someone continue to do something that hurts themselves and their loved ones? Why do they run through these stop signs? This chapter will explain all the factors that influence SUD people to continue their self-destructive behavior. Let us start with the brain.

Neuroscience

We are going to give some basic information to gain some understanding of what role the brain plays in substance abuse. The brain is like a supercomputer. It spreads information throughout our body, coordinating all body parts to function effectively. It continuously takes in data from the outside and uses that information to determine the course of action. Even while we sleep, our brain gathers information from the environment. The flow of information always continues. Our brain is constantly processing information and learning from experiences and interactions.

One of the functions of the brain is to seek out pleasure. That may sound hedonistic, but this is important if you think about it. Knowing what experiences are pleasurable and which are not can help us manage our daily routines. If we encounter a pleasant interaction, that will direct our actions. We will want to repeat that action that led to the good feeling. How much we enjoy an interaction influences social experiences, choices in food, and many other decisions. We seek enjoyable experiences and avoid unpleasant ones.

Any experience creates a chemical reaction in the brain. Neurotransmitters are chemical messages the brain sends to the rest of the body. They are necessary to maintain communication between the brain and the body. Endorphins are our body's natural opioid. Serotonin stabilizes moods. Dopamine is a pleasure chemical. Neurotransmitters carry messages across synapses, the space between cells and specific receptors on the target cell. Which neurotransmitters are released depends on the experience and how we interpret that experience. Chemical reactions occur in a short burst or sustained release.

When we introduce drugs into our system, this creates the release of dopamine. This release is far greater than anything we naturally experience. Drug use can produce up to ten times the dopamine a person could experience having sex. Not only does a person experience intense feelings from drug use, but dopamine also reinforces a behavior. Individuals become motivated to repeatedly seek out this experience.

Our body seeks a homeostatic or balanced state. The brain detects the additional dopamine from the substance and shuts down its natural production. The neurotransmitters are changed by this process and adapt to the chemical (substance). Since balance is essential for maintaining homeostasis in all creatures, our body will not see the need to overproduce and will stop its production. In time, the person depends on the substance to produce this feeling. Motivation, learning, sleep, cognition, and moods are negatively affected when a person refrains from using substances. The brain becomes hijacked by substances, making it difficult to experience pleasure from anything besides substances. The obstacles can vary, but the longer someone is using substances and the more intense the experience, the more significant difficulties the user will experience in trying to stop their use.

The longer the use, the more tolerance the individual's body develops. Since the body adapts to the substance, the system stops independently working. It relies on the substance of choice to sustain itself. If an individual stops using substances, the experience will be unpleasant. In some cases, life-threatening. If the use has been going on for a while, getting advice from a doctor on stopping or tapering off the use becomes necessary. There are significant negative withdrawal symptoms derived from abruptly stopping substance use and these must be carefully considered.

Since the brain has already connected the pleasurable experience of substances, it commits that experience to memory. Anything that reminds them of that experience becomes a trigger or stimulus that awakens a memory of the pleasurable event. How the brain makes that connection is the trigger. The brain associates the "positive" feelings with that experience and triggers a physiological desire to repeat it. That is why we want to seek pleasurable sensations.

Motivation to stop using depends upon the strength of the triggers. The intensity of the triggers influences us. The more significant the trigger, the more overwhelming it can be to stop their use. Returning to the pre-substance use state requires time to reset. This reset may take months and sometimes years. This time will require the body to start finding its way back to pre-use functioning. Over time, individuals no longer rely on substances to feel normal, navigate challenges, and improve their problem-solving skills. Until this reset happens, their view on stopping and having to experience triggers and the effort it takes to resist them will influence their motivation.

Normal Feelings

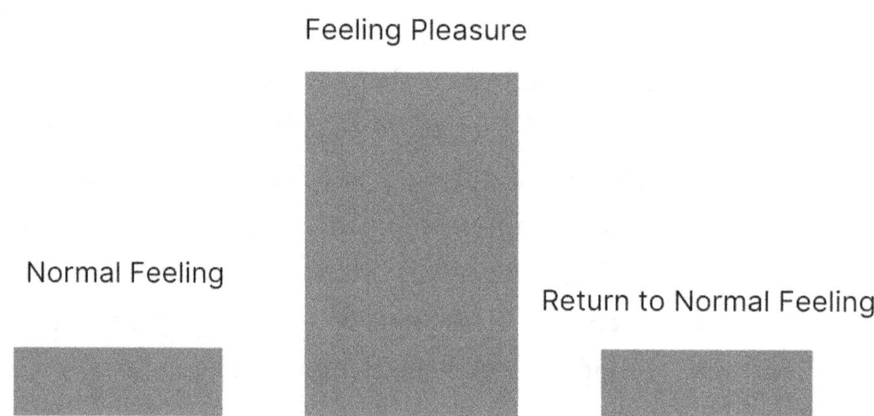

Individuals start out feeling normal. They have a pleasant experience and return to feeling normal

Occasional Substance Use

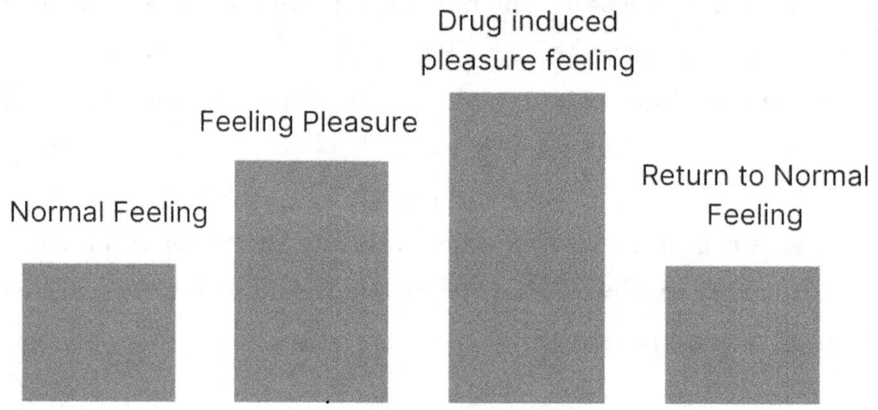

When someone uses substances, they are having a pleasant experience or feeling that normal experiences cannot match. The pleasant feeling is more intense.

Frequent Substance Use

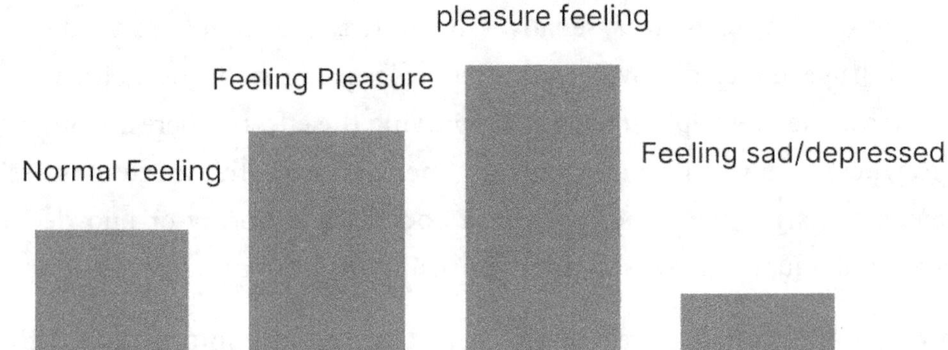

The more frequently the user uses substances, the less dopamine the user's body will produce. Since normal production of dopamine has slowed down or stopped, users will feel depressed once the effects of the substance wear off.

Using to Feel Normal

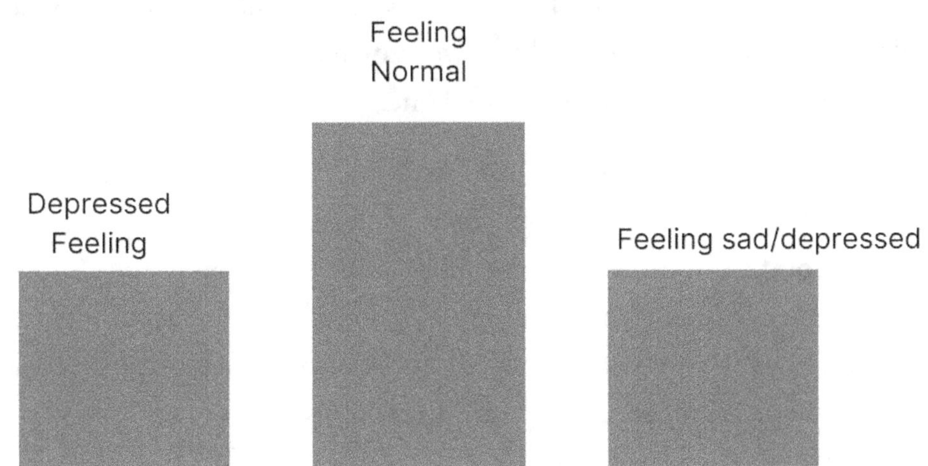

The longer the use continues, the more the user's body depends on the drugs for dopamine. When the effects of the drug wear off, they feel depressed. They come to rely on the substance to return to feeling normal as their dopamine production has shut down. The pleasure they received from earlier use is no longer obtainable.

Self-Medicating

Another challenge to consider in early recovery is the abuse of prescription drugs. Ideally, this will not happen if the prescribing doctor effectively manages the medication and any associated pain. The prescriber needs accurate patient information. Unfortunately, this is not always the case. For many reasons, a person can find themselves abusing prescription drugs. The most misused drugs include opioids, anti-anxiety medicines, sedatives, hypnotics, and stimulants. Adding recreational drugs and alcohol will make the prescription ineffective, either needing to increase the prescription drug or amplifying the effects. There are other situations where family or friends share their medications with the intent of assisting someone. Sharing medicines without a doctor's monitoring or knowledge will put an individual at increased risk of misusing the prescription.

Prescription drug users are not only reluctant to share information with their doctor and family regarding their misuse, but they will go to extraordinary means to protect themselves from having their medications taken away from them. When doctors cut back on refilling the prescription or limit refills, patients may seek recreational substances to compensate. Patients become dependent on the medicine. They will be defensive and protective if they perceive that their medication will be changed or stopped. Physical as well as psychological dependence on the drug develops. A family may see a problem with the person's use and align themselves against the doctor to support their loved one.

Individuals experiencing a mental health problem (depression, anxiety) or complex life events (divorce, loss of job) can turn to substances for relief and the perception of comfort. Substance use creates different effects on people. If someone is depressed, they may shift to substances to minimize the impact of the depressive symptoms. The high, though temporary, can allow them a reprieve or break from their symptoms or problems. They turn to the substance of choice to get through rough moments.

If people rely on the substance to manage rough moments, they use the substance as a coping tool. Once they stop their use, the mental health symptoms resume and the user continues to be ill-equipped to manage their mental health problems, their use independently, and the issues created by the substance use. It is common for those stopping their substance misuse to find themselves with significant emotional challenges. As we've discussed previously, substance abuse can mask mental health issues or, in some cases, exacerbate symptoms.

Self-medicating a mental health issue with substances prevents the user from recognizing problems. The use and symptoms develop simultaneously as the substance use (dual diagnosis or co-occurring disorder). Even experienced clinicians can miss co-occurring diagnoses. They may focus on one problem and not see the other.

As users become more dependent on substances to manage emotions (consciously or unconsciously), they lose their ability to cope without substances. They fear stopping as they understandably want to avoid the pain associated with their mental health problems. It is not only genetics that factor into mental health and substance issues but traumas and stress as well. The longer the problem and substance abuse continue, the more difficult it will be to manage both.

Lifestyle and Peers

In addition to the physical effects being complex, changing a lifestyle that revolves around substances could be even more challenging. These lifestyle changes involve not only social events and activities but friends or peers as well. If someone lives in a neighborhood where people often get together and partake in substance use, returning to that environment and maintaining sobriety will be difficult. Almost all recreational pursuits factor into this problem. Sporting events, either as a spectator or participant, often include alcohol use. For some, drinking and sporting events go hand in hand.

People associate with peers who they want to feel comfortable being around. We share common interests and enjoy that connection. We choose our associations to feel supported. It is essential to feel a part of something. If someone's circle of friends includes heavy users, going against the norms of that group (heavy use) will be difficult. The group may not aggressively encourage you to use substances with them. The recovering user's fear is losing connection with the group. Sometimes, the group can feel uncomfortable or threatened by someone stopping their use. Heavy users, at some point, will give some thought or consideration to stopping their use. If one of the people in a group stops their use, group members may be forced to reflect on their patterns. If they're trying to decide whether they have a problem with their own use, having a peer stop will bring that to the forefront of their thoughts.

A similar peer group allows the substance user to avoid seeing their use as a problem. It has the effect of insulating them. Their peers will help minimize the problems. They will also serve as reference points. The patterns established by their group will be used as a general reference overall.

A good example is teenagers. Most teenagers who smoke marijuana will declare that everyone in high school smokes marijuana. However, most statistics present that a small percentage of high school students actually engage in marijuana use. The peer groups they associate with and connect with will tell them otherwise. Their perceptions are different from reality. Suppose they perceive that most high school students smoke marijuana. In that case, it is understandable that it would influence their lack of motivation to stop.

A subculture exists when a group establishes norms, beliefs, and routines that are different or unique. The members share common interests and ideas. Examples of subcultures include ethnic, religious, recreational pursuits, gender, and musical, to name a few. Substance users form their subculture as well. They develop attitudes and behaviors around their substance misuse. They feel comfortable and safe in this group. They are accepted and have a sense of belonging. This bond can be substantial. Adolescents in a substance use subculture will be protective of their group. Finding an identity and establishing peer groups are essential developmental tasks during adolescence. Breaking away from this group will be difficult. Staying with the group and not using substances would be even more difficult.

For adults, this is not any easier to break away from peers with whom they have long-established relationships. Ironically, the more their use alienates family members, the greater the likelihood that the individual finds comfort in the group that supports the problem. The group reinforces the belief it is not the drugs or alcohol but the family members that are making life difficult. The peers insulate them, in some respects, from the consequences of their using substances.

Emotions influence behavior. The fear of change or leaving something meaningful (substance use) behind creates stress. Often, users feel shame about how they got into this circumstance. They may feel hopeless if they see leaving their use behind as near impossible. Concern over the loss of friends or recreational pursuits tied to using is a factor. Anger also tends to be present for a variety of reasons, mainly that others expect them to stop using substances (anger at themselves, the substances, or the family for making these demands on them). They become confused about the difficulties of quitting. Users often become pessimistic at trying to repair relationships damaged by the use. They experience fear and doubt about their ability to make the necessary changes.

In describing the hurdles users face, we are not giving the person a free pass for their misuse. We are only pointing out how difficult it can be for users to stop. SUD is a self-feeding disease. The further along it goes, the more ingrained the use becomes. The more consequences present, the more their support systems distance themselves. Users isolate themselves from individuals who can help them. If additional outcomes occur, such as job loss, the user increasingly finds they have fewer resources for sobriety. They will turn to peers who support their use. This fear tends to drive the user back to the peer group who already accepts them and their use.

The family must accept that to navigate the challenges, the situation may and often does temporarily worsen after they stop using. That would be the middle of the road, a decision point where the user decides down which road to proceed. This is a tough point in the sobriety journey. Tough sacrifices, lifestyle changes, and repair of relationships are among the tasks they need to navigate as they begin the journey toward home.

Individual family members negotiate where they fit into the user's recovery plan, and that may depend upon the user's motivation to end the negative consequences. For example, choosing to reassure family members, becoming transparent about where they have been and what they have been doing, explaining their actions to family members, or using a breathalyzer, proactively provide reassurance to family members, especially if lying was previously an issue.

It's the Middle Part That Sucks!

Most of what we have covered addresses how to manage staying in or recovering from a relationship that is impacted by SUD. Unfortunately, some relationships and families are not able to remain intact. Staying in a relationship with someone who is actively abusing substances may present concerns or risks that require someone to consider ending their relationship. It may be the healthiest option for some families. Knowing that leaving is an option is helpful for those individuals who feel stuck or left with limited choices.

Individuals hope for healthy relationships. Initially, relationships may work because some benefits are derived from the connection, but eventually the substances become destructive. The more intense the benefits received, the more likely the user is to ignore the consequences. The longer they are in this association, the more difficulty they experience in separating from it. This connection does not have to be just with a person. It could exist in a situation such as work or a thing such as a substance. Substance users struggle with the same challenges as those in an unhealthy marriage or romantic relationship.

Families will recognize the problems associated with a loved one who is a substance user. Some part of them realizes the relationship with the user is causing them emotional, physical, or psychological harm, while another part of them wants to pretend harm is not happening. From the outside looking in, it is easy to become frustrated when observing those unable or unwilling to escape it. Regardless of the problem, those outside the relationship will see the situation differently than you do. They will have less of an emotional investment than you will.

Individual family members intellectually understand the problem they face. Emotionally, they struggle with how to manage the situation. At times, they may understand the perspective of the user. Unfortunately, these insights can be short-lived, and the individual quickly retreats to the "safety" of their unhealthy relationship. People can be so overwhelmed at the prospect of change and what is involved that they may believe it is safer to stay in the relationship. Why would someone stay in an unhealthy relationship even though it is costly? The perceived benefits they receive from staying where they are often outweigh the challenges they face in leaving it.

For family members, it is based on fear of being alone, finances, or concern about the impact on children. Those are usually the typical reasons why they may choose to stay. For others, it might not be the right time in their life to undertake such a move.

It is helpful to remember that even though a relationship may cause distress and problems in a person's life, it serves a function. For many, it feels good to continue the relationship even though feeling and being good are not always the same. What feels good is not always good for us. An example is chocolate cake. It tastes good but may be problematic for those trying to lose weight. Substance use is another example. The momentary satisfaction they receive outweighs their desire to change. Not leaving serves a function, giving the appearance of feeling safer to stay than go.

This function makes it difficult for them to change. A family member's reluctance is further fueled by previous unsuccessful attempts to get out of the relationship. The reality of the challenge that lies ahead for them can be overwhelming. Their confidence is shattered, and they fall back into the safety of what is comfortable to them. The perceived benefits of not changing outweigh the benefits of leaving. The situation becomes even more difficult if they present the desire to leave but then return to the using person. They have lost the support system that would have fostered their change. They may also lose their confidence in their ability to make any changes.

Staying with a substance user may seem like an unhealthy choice. However, there are many reasons for staying with an active substance user. The choice to stay can be based on timing. Financially, a person may not be able to afford the costs of living on their own. The children may be in a fragile state and a divorce would have a huge impact on them. A loved one may not be in an emotional position to face the stress of leaving--they are just not ready to leave yet.

Families can recognize that their loved one is struggling with a substance use problem. They can recognize that their relationship with the user is unhealthy. As a result, deciding to leave the relationship can be challenging and infused with intense emotions. Those looking at the relationship from the outside, like extended family members or friends, may feel it makes sense for the loved one to leave the substance user. However, it's not that simple. The family member's history with the user and the feelings they have for them add to the difficulty of making this decision.

You may find yourself in a transitionary period of realizing a change needs to be made. It may take time to plan and develop the resources you need to move on. You recognize that you're better off leaving but are overwhelmed by the journey you will be taking. Your focus is gaining the confidence in facing the challenges that accompany the decision to leave. Acknowledging that the middle part of a journey is just that—an in-between time—is helpful. Your focus is on the path you've chosen to take, leaving the relationship, and facing the challenges that come with it. It's not unusual for you to feel ambivalent, or to go over in your head the pros and cons of being in or out of the relationship.

Once you believe that moving forward is the correct decision, you can focus on making the transition as comfortable and manageable as possible. For example, if you're on a road trip from the Midwest to the West Coast of the US by car, the road is mundane for many travelers. Focusing on the destination allows the traveler to tolerate the boring parts of the journey. Preparing and planning for the middle part makes the trip more manageable. Let's look at some examples of how to make the transition easier.

Notes for the Journey Home

In this middle part between acknowledging we're in an unhealthy relationship and actually leaving the relationship, we need to look at some practical ways to prepare for the challenges of a direction change. For some, this may mean developing new friendships or support systems. We **need** friends who will be supportive of the goal of leaving that relationship. A strong safety net should be in place to help us in the difficult transition.

Fostering new recreational pursuits and focusing on health through diet or exercise are also helpful ways to care for ourselves during this transition. Develop an action plan with the end goal in mind. The better we prepare for transitioning out of a relationship (middle part of the journey), the less turbulent that transition will be.

Other resources for the journey ahead include counseling and support systems. They are invaluable in providing emotional encouragement to know you're not alone. Support groups or religious organizations can also be helpful. The important thing to remember is that you won't experience this set of circumstances forever. This is a temporary time of transition on your way to a better life. It is a means to an end that will lead to a destination healthier than the substance using relationship.

- **If you're concerned about finances,** consumer credit counseling agencies offer guidance. They can help you develop a budget and consolidate loans.

- **Legal matters also need to be considered.** Legal advice is available through a variety of services including community or religious organizations.

- **Determine which family and friends will be supportive.** Surround yourself with those who support your decision.

- **Look for support groups with people facing similar obstacles.** Religious and community resources are readily available.

- **Engage in recreational pursuits.** Check your local park district or meetup groups (www.meetup.com).

- **Consider joining a gym.** Paying attention to your health and healthy pursuits empowers you through a difficult time. Small changes can significantly improve our moods.

- **Recognize your self-talk.** How you view your situation and the things you say to yourself can either help or hurt you. At times, you may feel discouraged. Remember, this is the middle part of the journey (which sucks). There will be an end, which will lead to a better position.

- **If there is domestic violence, please seek help.** Most communities have services for those in abusive situations. Leaving is a sensitive time and requires additional support to provide a safe environment.

Many choices are available for help on this journey. Consider all of them. If you decide to leave, create a safe supportive environment. Remember why you embarked on this journey. For a better future, a better life for yourself.

· · · · · ·

CHAPTER 3

Impact on the Family

· · · · · ·

**"Addiction is a family disease. One person may use,
but the whole family suffers."**

~Author Unknown

Families encounter substance use disorders as a family unit and as individuals. While the family experiences substance use together, they also each respond in their own way to the situation. Substance use changes the way one thinks and behaves. In the family context, repeated and increasingly excessive use requires family members to make their individual changes that support the user's behavior.

When families function well, family members have roles and responsibilities and can care for one another's needs. As a substance use problem progresses, the user spends more time acquiring, using, or recovering from their use, which requires family members to compensate. Much like a mobile over a baby's crib, the distinct parts of the family move and strike a balance. Substance use throws the mobile off balance, and family members attempt to create balance again. The stress of doing so takes its toll on the family.

Abuse, Neglect, and Trauma

Substance use affects the functioning of the family. According to SAMSHA, one in eight children under the age of 17 grow up in a home with substance abuse, an estimated 8.7 million children (about half the population of New York) (3). In addition, 39.1 percent of children removed from their home for child abuse or neglect in 2021 had substance abuse as a condition for their removal from their home as reported by the Adoption and Foster Care Analysis and Reporting System (AFCARS). This can be traumatic and increases the likelihood of developing a substance abuse disorder later in life (4, 5, 6).

Abuse and neglect have far-reaching consequences. Studies between 1995 to the present have linked long-term health problems to 10 Adverse Childhood Events (ACEs), including:

- Physical abuse
- Sexual abuse
- Emotional abuse
- Emotional neglect
- Physical neglect
- A mentally ill, depressed or suicidal person in the home
- Drug-addicted or alcoholic family member
- Witnessing domestic violence against the mother
- Loss of a parent to death
- Loss of a parent to abandonment
- Parental divorce
- Incarceration of any family member for a crime

The studies found that stress in children impacts their bodies and minds through prolonged release of cortisol (the stress hormone). This exposure to dangerously elevated levels of cortisol affects children's ability to learn, creating a greater risk for academic failure and an increased likelihood of medical illness throughout their lifetime (7, 8, 9, 10).

Those with substance use disorder often experience higher rates of infidelity, domestic violence, child abuse, child neglect, sexual abuse, codependency, and other dysfunctional relationship patterns. Additional effects on the mental and behavioral health of families might include phobia, fear of abandonment, interpersonal sensitivity, anger outbursts, problems with verbal skills, and the development of other family members' substance use disorders.

Trauma exposes a person's nervous system to extremely elevated levels of stress hormones, and this chronic exposure leads to a heightened stress response. Someone who has *not* experienced traumatic events responds with a **temporary** increase in their stress reaction. The individual *with* trauma exposure experiences **extended episodes** of heightened stress response that tends to leave the person locked in a state of fight, flight, or freeze. Individuals who experience trauma become hypervigilant, always expecting the unexpected. They lose a sense of stability and predictability. They are always in survival mode. Their reactions and interactions can be intense, or they may underreact to stress (11, 12).

The Family Finds an Unhealthy Balance

Substance use disorder becomes all-consuming and destructive to one's most personal relationships, especially with family members and close friends. Substances change the way one thinks and behaves, causing the family to feel and act differently in support or alternately in reaction to the substance user. As the user maintains their use, and the family consciously or unconsciously supports it. Substance use also creates patterns of emotional instability that impact the functioning of the family and the individuals within the family. Family members' relationships in and outside the home are fundamentally changed.

Families develop behaviors and feelings to cope with difficult circumstances that worked to manage their life in a dysfunctional traumatic family setting. Eventually, these behaviors no longer serve us as adults. These include:

- Difficulty trusting other people

- Chronic loneliness

- Lying

- People pleasing

- Intense self-criticism

- Increased likelihood of developing substance issues

- Accepting responsibility for the choices and behavior of others

- Fear of abandonment

- Shutting down when stress becomes overwhelming

- Perfectionism

- Executive dysfunction

- Feelings of inadequacy

- Feel the need to rescue others

- Hypervigilance

Finding a way through traumatic experiences and dysfunction brought about by substance use disorder requires a commitment to changing the trajectory of events that have occurred in a family. Repair and healing are possible. It requires honesty, transparency, and communication that is uncomfortable for the substance user and the family. This is different than how family members were conducting themselves while the use was active. When use was occurring, families did what they needed to maintain balance. Honesty, transparency, and communication, although healthy pursuits, are compromised by the situation. Some families have been damaged beyond repair; others overcome tremendous dysfunction to find a new way to live together.

Parental Internal Conflict

Parents provide care for their children through support, guidance, love, direction, and a home for the kids to grow into responsible, independent adults. That role becomes complicated, if not impossible, to carry out when substance abuse is involved. SUD affects everyone who is in proximity to the user. Children are particularly vulnerable. Family members will feel the emotional impact of the energy spent in addressing the addiction. Children's emotional and physical safety is jeopardized. If a parent is experiencing substance abuse problems, the impact is felt by all family members. The ability to carry out parenting responsibilities and provide a nurturing environment for a child is diminished.

People who experience addiction become consumed with avoiding the consequences of their use and still feel the need to use. Children who observe this playing out in their family will see and experience the conflict. Children will be aware of the stress the addiction presents in the family. The younger children may be unable to articulate what is happening, but they know something isn't quite right. The using parent realizes the stress their use is causing others. They make excuses to rationalize their behavior. The user deflects, avoids, and denies, minimizing the impact of their use. This allows the use to continue.

This occurs because of what is known as *cognitive dissonance*. Cognitive dissonance is when someone holds two conflicting values, attitudes, behaviors, or beliefs at the same time. Normally, our brain does not allow this to happen. If we behave in a way that conflicts with our values, we feel emotional discomfort. Conflict exists that needs to be rectified.

An example of this is someone who steals from a department store. The person sees something they like and takes it without paying for it. Although the individual sees themselves as honest, their action of stealing conflicts with this belief. To reconcile this, they rationalize it. "Stores make such a profit, so it's not a big deal," or "I've spent enough money at this store, so they owe me."

The substance abuser justifies their actions in the same way. They engage in denial to avoid recognizing their own cognitive dissonance. They tell themselves. "I don't have a problem. I don't use substances as much as other people. It's not that bad. Everyone is just overreacting." This type of self-talk allows the user to continue their substance abuse. By engaging in this type of self-talk, the user doesn't have to face the guilt or shame from their use. Justification allows them to avoid the consequences of their use and they can leverage this against any fears that it would be difficult to stop using. Denial is a defense mechanism that maintains the belief that alcohol or drugs are not a problem. It protects them from the reality that their behavior is problematic to others. They will reject new or opposing information that conflicts with their beliefs and behavior. Drinking and driving are good examples of this. Forty-three percent of Americans admit to drinking and driving when it is well-documented that driving and drinking is unsafe. They may justify it with "It's only a short distance. What's the big deal" (14).

If a child sees their parents having problems created by their substance use and is told by the parent that what they see is not a problem, the child experiences dissonance. Either the child trusts what their parents tell them (use is not a problem) or they don't believe their parents. Parents who they rely on for direction tell them something they see is not what they see. There are two conflicting thoughts. For the child to reconcile this, they must either agree with the using parent or turn against that parent. This can lead to a lack of confidence in their ability to believe in their own judgement or observations.

Shame and embarrassment create other feelings for a child in this position. The child of a substance abuser recognizes there is an unhealthy situation at home. Avoidant behaviors develop such as not bringing friends home, keeping away from the house, or staying in their room. Isolation becomes how they cope. Children of users also feel guilty over their parent's use, believing they can somehow control or stop the use.

Anger is another common emotion experienced by children. They may see what is occurring at home and get angry with the addicted parent. In other situations, they rally behind that parent and support the using parent's efforts at minimizing the behavior or denying the problem.

If the user commits to abstinence, the child doesn't automatically reset their emotions about the situation. Events that transpired while the use was occurring leave a mark and must be processed as a family. Essential dialogues are needed to address the emotions and circumstances around the use. If not, the emotions and struggles carry into adulthood and into other relationships the child will experience in the future. Aside from a strong genetic link in families with addiction, there is a learned component. Both factors contribute to the higher likelihood that kids who come from substance abusing families will be at elevated risk of developing problems themselves (15).

Isolation is also common in SUD families, produced by shame, embarrassment, or the user's manipulation. In some cases, the user alienates friends and family to avoid a threat to their use. External events, such as observing the user repeatedly drunk or high in public, a DUI, or a job loss due to using behavior, are typically motivating factors to encourage users to stop their substance use. Families frequently isolate themselves from others to avoid exposure. By not bringing outsiders home and limiting time with them, users ensure those outside the family only see what the user and family want them to see. This allows the use to continue unimpeded.

Notes for the Journey Home

There are long-term consequences to experiencing substance use within your family. Recognizing the impact of living with a substance user and the behaviors adapted within the family to cope with reality of life in a substance using household present some difficulties. Here are some things to consider as you prepare for the journey to recover as a family:

- **Your experience is valid.** Family members have been affected by the use within the family and have felt the consequences of the users' behavior.

- **You need healing as well as the substance user,** whether it's healing relationships or yourself. Be mindful of how you cope with the situation.

. . . .

CHAPTER 4

Commitment to a Journey

. . . . . .

"Sobriety is a journey, not a destination."

~Unknown author

Defining a goal for SUD is essential not only for the user but for family members as well. Goals provide us with direction and accountability. Imagine if you commit to losing 15 pounds. You develop a plan to decrease calories, increase water intake, and exercise consistently. Your plan must have a specific target with a means to achieve your goal. Or, if your boss tells you he wants you to improve your performance at work, creating a plan to correct the problem is more effective if you understand what you need to accomplish. Now, suppose a user and their family agree on goals about moderation or abstinence. In that case, they work together to move in the same direction. But if they have different goals or agendas—to use or not to use—conflict will happen.

Defining Goals for the User and Family

A person with SUD struggles with giving up their use. It has become vital to them, and most often, they prefer to keep using despite the consequences. Individuals with SUD deny or minimize the impact of their use, get angry, or defensive. Some provide vague commitments to address the issue. Comments such as "I'll cut back" and "I'll slow down" or "I'll only use it on special occasions" are consistent with this mindset. Excuses avoid accountability and allow the SUD individual to circumvent committing to stopping their use. If someone drinks a case of beer daily, cutting back can be three six-packs and five beers daily. Unclear expectations such as that leaves both parties frustrated and disappointed. Technically, the individual is "cutting back," but the action falls short of the family's expectation.

While the use is active, the family doesn't discuss the use, ignoring incidents revolving around it, and picking up family responsibilities neglected by the user to do whatever they need to make sure the family system maintains itself. Direct discussion about the use creates pushback from the user. Expectations need to be clear for both parties once a common goal is determined (abstinence, moderation). In SUD families, candid discussions about the use typically don't happen. There's a silent agreement in families not to upset the status quo by confronting the user. This dynamic needs to change to allow families to negotiate new family rules and expectations. If there are setbacks (relapses), families may observe subtle changes in the user's behavior. Individuals and families need to determine if it is a decision to use versus a regression.

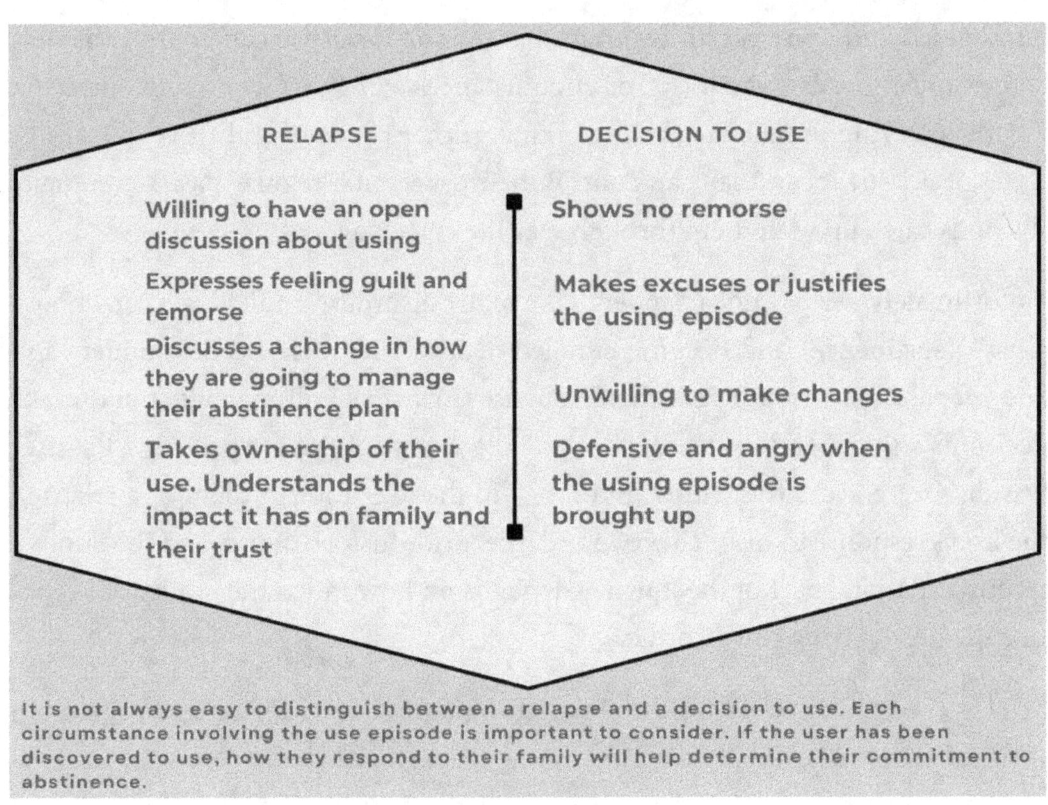

It is not always easy to distinguish between a relapse and a decision to use. Each circumstance involving the use episode is important to consider. If the user has been discovered to use, how they respond to their family will help determine their commitment to abstinence.

> "Remember, just because you hit bottom doesn't
> mean you have to stay there."
>
> *–Robert Downey, Jr.*

Abstinence vs Moderation

Suppose the user agrees to moderate their use. In that case, there should be a discussion regarding what to do if the user is not successfully limiting their use. Cutting back or limiting use is only realistic for some individuals. One or two successful weekends don't mean moderation is a productive route for recovery. If the use is significant, has been going on for a while, or there have been previous attempts at stopping, abstinence tends to be a more productive goal, especially if the user puts themselves or others at risk. If we walk across a busy street blindfolded and don't get hit by a car, that doesn't mean we can control the outcome. It just means we're lucky, or circumstances somehow worked in our favor. For those trying to manage their drinking, if they're successful three out of five times, it doesn't mean they can control their usage on a regular basis. Eventually the odds catch up with them through real-life consequences.

Unfortunately, relapse does happen. Like many disorders, individuals can choose a path (abstinence) and become derailed. Family members need to understand and prepare for a response if this happens. How they will manage it and make decisions will depend on factors such as the extent of the relapse, how the user was discovered (did the family find it or did the user inform them of a relapse), the user's response to his recovery or relapse, prior history of use, and the family's resources. A vital part of the journey depends on how much the family can separate the person from the disorder.

SUD is consuming. Users find themselves doing all sorts of things to maintain their substance use and often acting in ways that violate their value systems. Forgiveness won't come quickly or easily, particularly if families have experienced extensive consequences. Families will find themselves rebuilding their relationships on "pins and needles." Past conversations about their use may not have gone so well. If they're actively using substances, the user will dismiss concerns about use.

The long-term consequences of use may be harder to recover from than anticipated, especially if there has been violence. Financial recovery takes years to repair. Legal implications take both time and money.

Even if families and users are on the same page, discussing what to expect is necessary. We tend to look ahead to the day when sobriety will be easy and there will be no more fear. That's the result families want to see. However, the middle part can be rough. There will need to be some readjusting of responsibilities. If the family was compensating for the user and filling in gaps in parenting created by their use, the family reluctantly gives up their independence. The user may be frustrated in gaining back the trust and confidence of the family. Open dialogues are uncomfortable since defensiveness, shame, and guilt tend to be associated with SUD families. The family faced adversity and uncertainty due to SUD—some experienced chaos and trauma. A return to "normal" will take time.

Recovery

What direction conversations take will depend on the individual's motivation to change. If people don't want to modify their behavior or see the need to change, introducing tools or discussions to stop their use will be meaningless.

Users receiving a perceived benefit from substances often need external influences to create the catalyst to stop. If they receive perceived internal benefits (feeling good when using), they will continue to use them until outside factors (external) motivate them to change.

Motivation to Change

Mental health professionals use a model to address motivation with their clients. It is called the Transtheoretical Model (developed by Prochaska and DiClemente in 1984) (17). This model identifies four stages of change.

Stage 1: Precontemplation

People in this stage have no intention of changing their behavior. They have no purpose for change and don't see any negative consequences to their use.

User Actions	Family Actions
• Some discussion or identification that there's a problem. • There is no commitment to stop or slow down. • They're ambivalent about the consequences of their use.	• Discuss the consequences of their use and impact on the family. This discussion should be optional but offered when they're in the frame of mind to have a dialogue. • Continue to focus on the use, not the reasons or excuses they use. The reason they're having trouble with their substance use will come later. Now we look at how to stop using.

Stage 2: Preparation

At this stage, people are ready to act. They're open and willing to make changes. However, they have yet to approach how this will happen. They haven't committed to a decision.

User Actions	Family Actions
<ul><li>They will acknowledge there's a problem.</li><li>They aren't resistant to the idea of stopping.</li><li>They're not ready to act but identify the problem.</li></ul>	<ul><li>Families continue to have a dialogue with them about their use.</li><li>Acknowledge to them how hard it must be to stop. Here, you're continuing to identify the problem as their use.</li><li>Educate the family on substance use and support.</li><li>Offer support at this stage.</li></ul>

Stage 3: Action

In this stage, the user commits to a plan and is ready to act. They identify the problem and are willing to work toward developing an action plan.

User Actions	Family Actions
<ul><li>They identify a problem.</li><li>They acknowledge their need to change.</li><li>They're willing to make and discuss changes.</li><li>Actively participating in treatment plan and have a support system.</li><li>Seek out self-help or a support group.</li></ul>	<ul><li>The family should be a part of the discussions about their role in recovery.</li><li>There's open dialogue on specific aspects of recovery such as preparing for events and other situations that would be triggers for the user.</li><li>Seek out Al-Anon or Families Anonymous and Therapy.</li></ul>

Stage 4: Maintenance

In this stage, they have sustained their recovery and developed a routine supporting their healing. They're maintaining behavior conducive to changing their use of substances.

User Actions	Family Actions
• There is open dialogue about their recovery. It's time to talk about past transgressions. • They take ownership of their use. They're acknowledging and repairing the damage done by their use. The user is open to discussing their use's impact on others. • Continue with recovery plan. • The user has gained confidence in their ability to maintain their gains.	• Families (including the user) are more grounded in their respective programs. • Discussion should include past events and having candid conversations as an integral part of repair. • The user is more confident in their recovery and there is more directed talk of future events. • There's less focus on obtaining sobriety and more on repairing the family.

There can be fluctuations and relapses. It's common for some individuals to alternate between one stage and another. The length of each stage will depend on the circumstances. The individual make-up of the family and user, life circumstances, and previous history as a family with substance use will all be factors in how someone moves through these stages. Change is an individual and collective journey in substance use disorder.

A commitment to stop using is the beginning. The process of stopping use is less certain. At times, users continue to engage in substance abuse despite their agreement with the family. In that case, there will be a need to consider other approaches, such as more intensive services. Reaching decisions about treatment options requires as much support and deliberation as possible. Therapists provide resources and linkages to assist families in identifying support for their substance-abusing family members. Ideally, families can work together to develop and maintain a recovery plan. Resources including counseling services are available for all family members and necessary to address the effects of witnessing active substance use disorder. Support groups and self-help groups are helpful at any stage of the recovery process.

Slippery Slopes

Developing a recovery plan allows family members to openly discuss concerns. Since recovery is different for each person, each family's plan will be unique. One threat that may arise during this planning time are slippery slopes—events, places, people, or times that can create challenges or present risks for those in recovery. For example, planning to see a friend they formerly used with may feel comfortable for the user, but unfortunately the family may worry about such a meeting leading to a relapse. It would be helpful for the person to share a game plan to reassure the family they're aware of the risks involved and are prepared for the potential challenges. For the family, it will be comforting and validating. These discussions help to rebuild the trust lost in addiction.

It can be difficult for a user's loved ones to let go of the past, especially when the use has had a tremendous impact on the family. Trust is needed and may take time to reestablish. Changes in an individual and their recovery impact the family and the user. Events such as block parties, weddings, birthday parties, holiday traditions, etc., often involve using and will require special navigation tools. These events can be challenging for both the user and family members. Families will need to decide if they attend or not. These events can bring up unwanted memories for the user and the family. Recovery is a shared journey; these decisions should be discussed and planned together as a family. Families sometimes struggle to get on the same page because they desire to do things as they've always done them. The changes in substance use patterns lead to the need to change long-kept habits, routines, and rituals, which often lead to conflict.

Discussions around the use, especially in the pre-contemplative stage, should keep this in mind. The longer the debate, the more likely your anger and frustration will increase. When that happens, adrenaline is released in our bodies as our stress response is activated. Our senses react as if we're under attack. In these situations, our hearing improves as it has activated the fight or flight response. However, our ability to listen lessens as the logical part of the brain takes a back seat to our survival part of the brain. Individuals will be more focused on tone, the other person's affect, or particular words than the content of the discussion (argument) itself. To sum it up, the longer a debate continues, the less productive it becomes!

FIGHT, FLIGHT, OR FREEZE

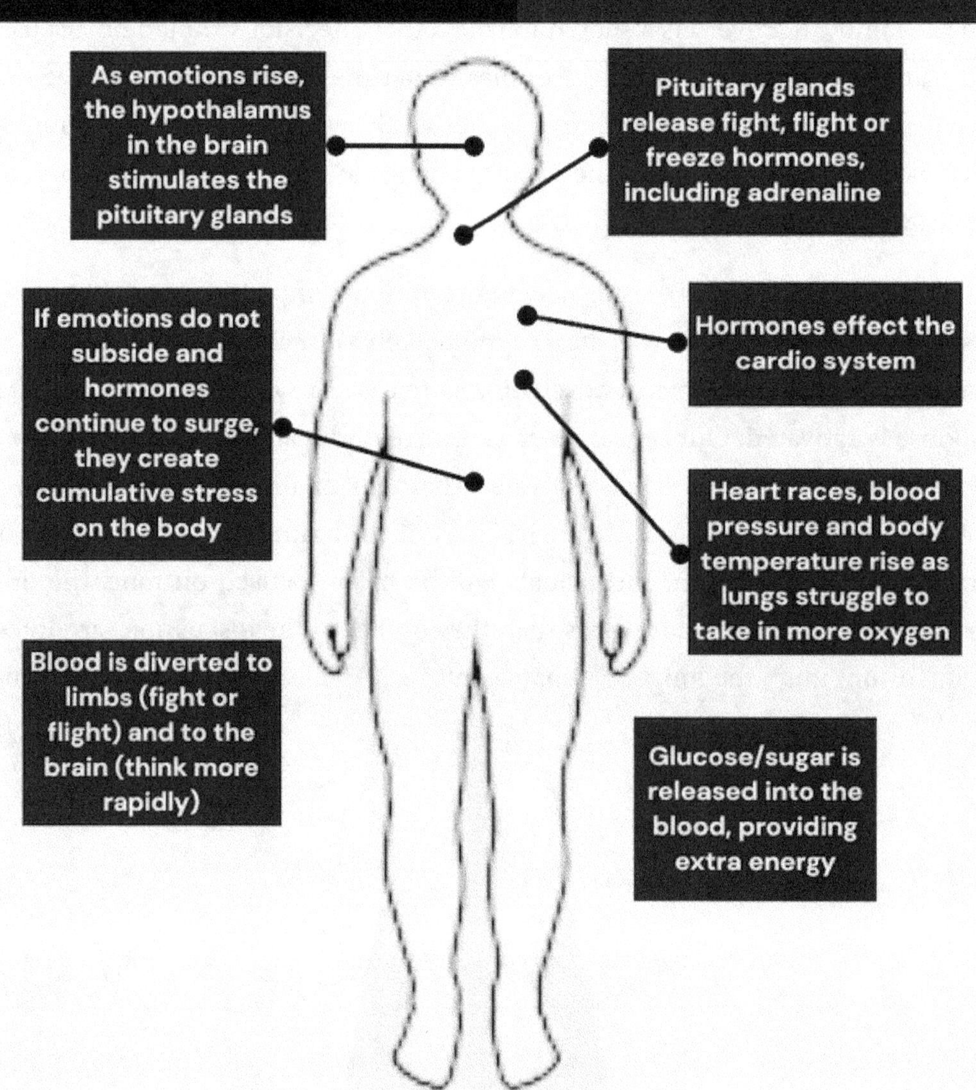

If the user continues to abuse substances, the family will need to make decisions. If an adolescent is using, the family needs to consider more intensive services. For adults, more intensive services, separation, or divorce may be considerations. Each decision will be challenging to work through. It would be nice for families to have a crystal ball to see when or if the misuse will end. Unfortunately, there is no such thing. You should seek the help and encouragement of as many support groups, therapists and other families as you can.

Notes for the Journey Home

Ideally, families can work together to develop and maintain a recovery plan. In most families, SUD is kept secret or not discussed. Growing up, kids may witness active substance use and not have anyone to talk about it with or anyone who even acknowledges the use as a problem. As uncomfortable as it may be, these discussions with children, even young ones, are essential. Children often feel responsible for the difficulties in a family, and the silence can reinforce these beliefs. Here are some suggestions to facilitate communication for families in recovery:

- **Focus on the use and its impact on the family.** Family members should not allow themselves to blame one another for the user's choices. They are not responsible for the person's use of substances.

- **Openly discuss triggers.** Discussing the trigger and situations that create the urge to use is productive. There should be a distinction between a user talking about his trigger and blaming the trigger or others' behavior for their use. For example, "You yelled at me, so I used." The alternative would be, "When we argue, I feel triggered. I made the choice to use."

- **Choose the proper time for a discussion.** If a person is under the influence, conversations about their use shouldn't occur during those times. Nothing productive will happen. Proactive conversations (prior to an episode) are more helpful than discussions after an event. Plan a sit-down dialogue, especially those that have the potential to become intense.

- **Choose appropriate settings.** Decide on environments that will feel neutral and safe for everyone.

- **Stop conversations that start getting heated.** If you're repeating points, you most likely have reached an unproductive place. Taking time out from discussions is okay instead of prolonging them and saying things you regret. Take a breather and reconvene at another time. Consider working with a therapist to help navigate discussions that are difficult.

- **Pursue their recovery as a joint effort.** Everyone wants the same thing: the family to be happy and heal from SUD. Allow all family members, when possible, to participate in the recovery.

- **Accept responsibility for mistakes.** Ownership of mistakes and missteps helps build relationships, for both the user and the family. It shows that we all have room for improvement and gives the user an added measure of feeling safe to share their struggles.

- **Avoid bringing up the past as much as possible.** There should be a discussion of the problem. However, the family will have difficulty healing if they keep circling over the things that happened in the past. They will be reliving the past and the hurt they experienced, constantly opening the wounds instead of healing. To be clear, letting go can be difficult. In the initial stages of recovery, there should be conversations about what occurred; however, discussions can reach a point where they are no longer productive. In later stages of recovery, bringing up the past can be counterproductive.

- **Stay on topic.** Families need to avoid "kitchen sinking arguments" (when we argue, we throw everything we can think of, including the kitchen sink, into the argument). This kind of discussion gets us nowhere and often leads to unresolved frustration and differences of opinion.

. . . . . .

CHAPTER 5

Addressing Change

. . . . . .

**"Healing doesn't mean the damage never existed.
It means the damage no longer controls our lives."**

~Unknown

For most people, change is difficult—even change that benefits us. Human nature, or wiring, prefers life to be predictable. Take, for example, someone who wins the lottery. Despite the financial windfall, not all players are happier after winning. Some lottery winners become suicidal or report feeling less optimistic than before winning the lottery. Although some people will feel hopeful about change, it still meets with resistance. There are many reasons why change is so hard, especially in families with SUD.

Neuroplasticity

A primary reason change is so difficult is that our brains are wired to protect us from change. We prefer things to be predictable. We've learned patterns and behaviors that become routines. Predictability allows us to prepare for challenges more efficiently. New situations are seen as threatening. To illustrate this point, we examine the brain.

Neuroplasticity is the ability of the brain to form and reorganize synaptic connections. It allows us to develop new lifestyle patterns. Initially, when faced with change, alterations in our actions go against the flow of existing patterns, or pathways. These neuropathways form as our brain develops. When we experience glitches or obstacles, we learn new ways to overcome them. The brain incorporates new learning over time and with repetition, essentially "rewiring" itself in new pathways. An experience is recognized and committed to memory; we do this for efficiency and survival. We will repeat the behavior and avoid others depending on the experience, whether it is pleasurable or painful. This process creates habits and routines. The longer and more often we engage in a behavior or thought, the stronger the pathway becomes. We react instinctively.

The longer the pattern has been established, the more travelled the path, the more difficult it is to change. Therefore, breaking these routines or patterns take some effort. For the SUD family, changing involves rewiring multiple routines and habits. The rewiring process for them may involve several factors including financial, emotional, and physical stressors impacting individual family members. Thus, taking on the task of confronting substance abuse seems monumental. For some families, simply keeping their heads above water is their primary focus.

As a result, they develop habits and routines that help them survive. Altering their course, even if the results appear beneficial, may initially require more energy. It can be difficult to consistently put in the day-by-day and moment-to-moment effort that leads to change. So, they choose the "road more traveled" pathways, even though the result leads to a return to use. This well-traveled road means putting their efforts into *not* changing and keeping life the way it was established during the substance use.

Families have established roles and routines necessary for their survival. Whether the change is integrating an SUD family back into their familiar roles or separating from them, they must alter and let go of behaviors that have allowed them to function. They're going in a direction that is either uncharted territory (i.e., leaving the user) or risky (i.e., trusting that the user is ready to take on the responsibilities).

Numerous relapses and broken promises factor into the resistance that families experience as they work to rewire their brains to trust again. Families will find allowing the user back into the family fold risky since the brain is wired to protect us and wants to avoid pain. The family unit experiences an imbalance as the user tries to reestablish their role and position in the family. The user may experience difficulty reasserting authority when the family has become used to managing on their own.

Choices and Consequences

There are three **choices** that families themselves face when their loved one is actively using substances: Change, adjust, or leave. The *change* part usually involves the user's participation. The user and the family work together to change the situation. The change involves the user's commitment to a path of recovery. All parties work to repair the damage. The second option is to *adjust*. If the user isn't committed to change or cannot modify their behavior, the family will look for their resources to manage their situation. They're not investing in repair and do not see themselves separating from the user. The last choice is the family deciding to *leave*. The two previous options are not viable for them, and they put their energy into leaving. Leaving could mean divorce, asking the SUD person to move out if they're of age, or moving out of a house where active use is occurring.

The **consequences** of substance use can vary from family to family. Thus, repair will be complicated and challenging. Families must decide if repair is an option in the case of these often-seen consequences:

- Domestic violence

- Physical abuse

- Sexual abuse

- Financial issues

- Infidelity

- Legal issues

Changing behavioral patterns will take time and patience. Families have found ways (some maladaptive) to manage the adversity of SUD. Even if unhealthy behavior patterns develop in response to SUD, the family may find comfort in repeating these behaviors. That's why children of alcoholics are at elevated risk for becoming a substance abuser (genetics also play a role) or being in a relationship with someone who misuses substances. Children from SUD homes are more likely to be neglected or abused (physically or sexually). Consequences such as these require healing. Unfortunately, the events associated with SUD are not always repairable and can turn into lifetime struggles.

When a family is experiencing SUD, inconsistent messages and behaviors occur. There is unpredictability and uncertainty. Families are unsure if they'll see the person they love or the erratic individual that substances control. A sober person will look and say different things than those under the influence. Families develop a type of early warning system that makes them hyper alert to subtle signs of use. This system may be overactive, making it difficult to distinguish if the user is trustworthy, even after they stop using drugs or alcohol.

The substance abuser will do whatever they can to protect their ability to continue using their substance. They become so convincing in their argument and defense that family members lose their confidence in themselves. This is called "gaslighting" and undermines the family's ability to recognize the signs of substance abuse. The user minimizes their use or denies it. The family notices something is wrong but doubts themselves. Further uncertainty arises if other family members don't speak out or acknowledge the substance use. Family members who see the use as a problem are both overtly and passively discouraged from discussing the misuse.

Children become hypervigilant and distrustful. If the user has made previous attempts to quit, children begin to doubt recovery is possible. They may ignore a relapse for fear of having to accept the parent has returned to using. They will distance themselves from the user to protect themselves. Children also distance themselves from the whole family to emotionally defend against the chaos, choosing instead to be at school or friends' homes.

"Loved ones did not **cause** the problem. The user will try to convince them otherwise. They cannot **control** it. Hiding their drugs and pouring out alcohol to prevent the user from drinking only makes the user angry. They cannot **cure** it."

~Al-Anon

Changing Behavior

Continued substance misuse creates conflicts with family and friends. The longer the substance misuse continues, the greater the impact it has on family and friends. These support systems become frustrated over broken promises and lies from the user. The user begins to hide their use once family members and friends actively disapprove of the drinking or drugs. Doing this protects their use, enjoyment of perceived benefits, and avoids consequences (confrontation). Friends and other family members get frustrated at the lack of movement for someone to do something about the person using. Not everyone understands how difficult it is for some people to leave these relationships or change someone else's behaviors. It is also unrealistic to feel that a family member can have that much control over someone to make them stop their use. As a result, support systems distance themselves from the family due to their frustration.

In the previous chapter, we discussed how important it is to establish clear goals with the user, as a family. "I'll slow down my use" and "I'll make sure it's not a problem" will not work. It is essential to agree on a common recovery language together. If abstinence is not the direction they choose and they're attempting to moderate their use, clear expectations need to be established by talking things through. What exactly does moderation look like?

Knowing the commitment being made by the user (abstinence vs. moderation) will help everyone to be on the same page. This prevents misunderstandings that may arise and helps regain family confidence in the recovering person. Openness and being direct are new but meaningful experiences in recovering families. It is essential families do not shy away from candid discussions; they are a crucial part of the repair work that is needed.

The "three Cs" are terms used in the recovery field. Loved ones did not **cause** the problem. The user will try to convince them otherwise. They cannot **control** it. Hiding their drugs and pouring out alcohol to prevent the user from drinking only make the user angry. They cannot **cure** it. The responsibility for stopping lies solely with the user. We cannot make someone stop using substances, but we can offer support and guidance to them.

The recovering person must accept full responsibility for their use and its impact on the family. That would be a primary goal to address in conversations. Once this happens, reestablishing trust and confidence in the user will take time, effort, and patience. All parties must recognize the use as a problem affecting everyone in the family.

3 C's of Recovery For Families

	Cause	Cure	Control
Myths families believe	The user implies the family causes their substance use. The family member believes they have caused the use and feels responsible for the user's recovery.	The family member believes they could cure the user from their substance use. They believe if they try hard enough, they could get the user to stop.	The family members believe their actions can control the user's decision to use. This could include actions such as hiding bottles of alcohol, taking away the car keys, and creating obstacles for the user.
Mistaken beliefs	The family member feels responsible for the user's decision-making. They believe the use of substances lies solely on the family member. The blame for use focuses on the family member and away from the user.	Trying to "cure" the user leads to frustration and hopelessness from the family member. They are looking for answers and cannot find them.	Loved ones will exhaust themselves to get the user to stop. They allow the user to escape the responsibility for addressing their use.
Thoughts to promote this belief	"It's my fault." "I need to stop doing things that upset my loved one because it makes them use."	"There has to be something I could do to stop my loved one's use." "I have to find an answer to my loved one's use."	"If I pour out the alcohol, they won't be able to drink." "I have to act so my loved one won't use."
Alternative perspective	The user is responsible for their own decisions. Family members can't choose for their loved one to use. Feeling guilty implies a family member did something wrong. If the loved one chooses to use, as painful as it is to see them decide to use, it's their choice.	Understandably, a loved one wants to alleviate the suffering of the user. Overcoming the challenge of a substance use disorder is not something that has an immediate cure or remedy. It will be a journey that needs to be led or directed by the user.	If the user can't control their use, it's unrealistic for the family member to believe they can. You cannot make someone do something they're not ready to do or don't want to do.

Realize that once the commitment to recovery happens, life doesn't instantly improve. New roles and expectations are being developed or former roles are being reestablished. Families need to understand they are on a journey. Further down the road, they will be better off. The middle part will be more manageable over time. Invest in the journey. If we recognize where we are and where we would like to be, the focus is not on looking back or forward but on what is in front of us—the middle road.

Conversations about the user's substance use will be challenging and awkward. However, they are essential. Keep in mind that open and honest discussions will take time. Addiction is a secretive illness. Often, it isn't talked about or acknowledged. The user fears that openly acknowledging their use will jeopardize their ability to continue use. There is ambivalence; part of the user understands they must stop. The other part wants to continue to use substances. If they don't talk about it, they hope they won't have to confront the possibility of having to stop.

Furthermore, they may feel ashamed to discuss or admit their problematic use. Users shape the family members' responses (denial, anger, avoidance) through anger or blame. The pattern allows the user to avoid discussing their substance use. Secrecy and SUD go hand in hand.

Another challenge families face in recovery is how to disagree with each other. Families experience disagreements; that is expected. *How* we differ is more important than if we dissent. The feeling of being heard—not agreeing with but hearing what the other person has to say—is essential to working out differences. When we believe we're under attack, real or perceived, our brain will tell us to respond in one of three ways: fight, flight, or freeze. It references previous interactions as a stressful or threatening situation and brings those reactions into the now. These reactions will take time to rewire in the brain, and subsequently how we react will take time to change as well. The more we discuss these obstacles before they happen, the more likely we can change them. The thinking part of our brain (prefrontal cortex) can help us minimize the emotional part (limbic system) from hijacking the conversation.

Finding your spot in a loved one's recovery is a difficult place. In recovery, there are limits to what role you can play. For a parent, realistically, if your child wants to be around people who use drugs, you cannot prevent that from happening. A parent could make it more difficult for their child to be around drug users (monitor their activities, not let certain friends in their house) but not stop them altogether. How and when to intervene requires some thought and a little bit of finesse. If the user wants to be around people who use substances, they will find a way. That doesn't mean you should open your house to their friends or allow substance use behavior to continue. Setting parameters and holding them accountable for their sobriety are essential. Having clear expectations and consequences is necessary. The hope is that the external barriers a family creates for the user can help steer them toward recovery.

Families need to be involved in their loved one's recovery. We cannot express enough how important it is for family involvement. We discussed the secrets, shame, guilt, frustration, and other challenges accompanying SUD. Sharing information about the journey in recovery will help all parties better understand each other's struggles. This type of open communication builds confidence and trust between family members.

Suppose someone is involved in a support group. In that case, the family can learn a lot from knowing what the support group offers and the member's experience. If the person in recovery is engaged in a 12-step program such as Narcotics Anonymous (NA) or Alcoholics Anonymous (AA), attending open meetings provides the family with context about substance use and its consequences. Periodic involvement of family members in individual therapy sessions allows the recovering user to address concerns that arise in recovery.

If a user is in therapy, therapists are required to keep conversations with their clients confidential. They cannot share what is said in session unless life-threatening circumstances exist. There should be no reason to exclude a family member from occasionally attending a session. It will be helpful for the therapist to offer the family members an opportunity to share their perspectives. Therapists can hear what other people say in a session without disclosing personal information their client shared in therapy. Considering all family members' views is a helpful method to rebuild trust and reassure family they share the same goals.

Lies and deceptiveness in SUD families are common. It will be reassuring that everyone knows what is happening in their recovery program. Participants can hear from the recovering individual about their struggles or triumphs. Sharing their recovery facilitates open conversations.

Lastly, recovering users do not always share with others when they relapse or return to active use, even with their therapists. Just because someone is attending therapy doesn't mean they're applying it productively. At times, users will withhold information, such as relapses, in sessions. There can be varied reasons for the user's decision (shame, not being committed to a recovery plan). Allowing family members to attend sessions (not regularly) will create more openness and accountability.

Family sessions will eventually be helpful as well. Those sessions will give the family more time and attention than occasionally sitting in on an individual session. Instead of a personal focus, this type of therapy focuses strictly on the family. Both will be helpful in the family's recovery.

Codependency

Another term used in addiction (and mental health) is codependency. Numerous books and support groups address this concern. Codependency is a term used for the continual adjustments families make on behalf of the user.

In a SUD family, codependents feel responsible for preventing the user's relapses or use. The user blames them for the fall from their recovery plan. The codependent will buy into the assignment of blame or the argument. An unhealthy cycle develops in which the focus is more on the family member than the user. The user escapes accountability, and the codependent feels responsible.

Hallmarks of codependency:

- You feel responsible for the behavior and emotions of others.

- You allow blame to be directed at you for someone else's actions.

- You have a strong need for approval from people.

- You regularly put others' feelings before your own.

- You apologize for someone else's actions and behaviors.

- You feel uncomfortable doing something for yourself.

- Others' moods strongly influence your mood.

- You avoid conflict or confrontation.

- You have a tough time saying no or setting limits.

- You have a powerful desire to make others happy.

- You're in a one-sided relationship. You're the giver, and the other person isn't trying from their end.

If you recognize yourself in some of the points above, that means you likely have developed this adaptation to cope with the stress of your home life. You have learned to manage life by taking care of others. Although this may seem noble on the surface, it is an unhealthy, fear-based response in an attempt to control your environment. And it has the potential to damage your relationships.

If you want to have healthy relationships going forward, breaking this cycle is of utmost importance. Giving up codependent behavior can be scary. As the user recovers, this way of coping is no longer productive and healthy for anyone. We suggest looking at support groups such as Adult Child of Alcoholics (ACOA), Al-Anon, or Families Anonymous (FA) for help and understanding. Finding a therapist or support group that addresses these issues will help the family member and the person in recovery.

Families experiencing SUD challenges lose themselves. They are off-balance and struggle to manage the situation as well as their own emotions regarding the problem. Day-to-day survival can be difficult. During the early part of recovery, emotions will be intense. The user will be adjusting to life without substances and facing the consequences of their use.

Notes for the Journey Home

It is essential to understand the difference between the process and the results in recovering from substance use. Plans change and need to be adapted. Success is not guaranteed, and flexibility is often necessary. Effective planning improves outcomes. How you address the use can influence but not MAKE someone stop using. That will always be their choice (remember the three Cs). Here are some suggestions to address SUD with an active user:

- **Confront them when they are sober.** You will not accomplish anything but frustrate yourself if you try to discuss matters when they're impaired.

- **Be mindful of how you present your thoughts.** Shame is not a good motivator. Most users experience some level of shame, so that will be counterproductive.

- **You can offer consequences.** Make sure you let them know what you plan to do if they continue using—and that doesn't necessarily have to mean leaving them. Explore other options. Whatever families decide, they must be sure they can back it up or implement it.

- **Listen to what the SUD person is saying.** In some cases, the user feels powerless over their use. Understand there is a difference between "I won't stop" and "I can't."

- **Remain calm.** Say what you have to say, then listen to the recovering response. Avoid repeating yourself. The longer an argument continues, the more likely you are to try to win the discussion rather than get your point across. Write down a bullet list of your concerns to refer to. This will help you keep a train of thought and not get sidetracked.

- **Be honest.** Lying or holding back information won't accomplish anything. Let the user know how their use is truly affecting you.

- **Align with other family members.** Find out if they have the same concerns as you. Plan out how you all can present a consistent message.

- **Present your concerns with empathy,** especially if other family members are involved. You don't want them to feel you're complaining about them and their use.

In the process of finding your way home, change occurs when one person decides to approach the situation in a different manner. If any member of the family decides to get help, modifies their behavior, or adapts their thinking or approach, the family is fundamentally changed. The differences may be seen in minute increments over time, but this process can have a tremendous impact.

Family Patterns Worksheet

Family patterns are routine ways in which we interact with our family. For example, when children were little, they would run and hide when Dad came home. He would walk in the door and yell "Where is everybody?" The kids would giggle from their hiding places, then run out to say, "Here I am!"

In the SUD family, there are patterned interactions that regularly occur. One client shared, "There was this air of foreboding when my dad walked in the door. Would he be angry Daddy or funny Daddy?" This is a common experience for families that experience substance use disorder. Even after the substance use ends, families carry those feelings of expectation and fear into other interactions. To change patterns, we need to recognize and rewire them.

Name three negative patterns of interaction in your family.

1. ____

____

2. ____

____

3. ____

____

What feelings are created by these interactions? (E.g., sadness, anger, fear)

____

____

____

What would be an ideal outcome? ("We could stop having the same argument.")

____

____

____

Negative family interactions create expectations that become routine when reinforced over time. Each time we engage in the same pattern, we create the likelihood we will repeat the pattern. Interrupting the pattern repeatedly creates the circumstances for wiring our responses.

Use your examples from above to create a new response. Think about the potential opportunities to interrupt the pattern.

- Change the thoughts.

- Change the response.

- Choose a behavior (as a family) to interrupt the pattern.

- Reframe negative thoughts with positive or neutral thoughts.

- Choose a different action.

Describe how this might look for you.

CHAPTER 6

Triggers for the User and Family

**"The best time to plant a tree was 20 years ago.
The second best time is now."**

–Chinese Proverb

Imagine you're walking through the forest. The trees are green and there's a gentle breeze blowing through the leaves. You walk down the path. You feel calm, peaceful. The birds are chirping, and you're in no particular hurry to get where you're going. Suddenly, you're face to face with a large bear. Immediately, your brain and body respond to the threat.

What is a trigger?

A trigger is a strong, negative emotional reaction to an event, action, or situation. The event, action or situation reminds the person of a traumatic or intense experience that is disturbing to them in some way.

Triggers are not voluntary. A person, place, thing, event, time, or even a smell can bring up involuntary memories from a previous situation. The reminder depends on a person's intense feelings regarding the stimuli. For the user, this feeling could be excitement and anticipation of reusing the substance. A trigger for the user doesn't mean they'll use or even want to use it. It just means that their brain has connected something to an intense experience (the sensation of being under the influence), and they're emotionally responding to it. For the family, they will also have triggers. These triggers will present feelings of anger, hurt, and fear.

What's happening inside the body when a trigger occurs? From a physiological perspective, a trigger is a stimulus that creates a response or reaction in a person by initiating a chain reaction within their brain and body. Each time a triggering occurs, it develops a neural pathway in the brain and, over time, shortcuts develop that allow the body and brain to respond quickly to stimuli. All responses that humans experience are encoded with a neural pathway that becomes more efficient with the intensity, frequency, and duration of the pathway.

The brain's responses become so streamlined that they don't appear to have a logical association with the trigger. For instance, most people won't feel stressed when they hear a specific song. Another person will have difficulty hearing that song if it reminds them of a failed romance. In substance use, something as simple as a beer commercial can be a trigger. Events that were typical use times such as a wedding, family gathering, or a stressful day, to name just a few, become triggers. This could be anything that reminds you of past substance use.

Despite the negative consequences associated with using substances, users can have difficulties with urges to return to their use. The desire Ito use is due to the strong neurological, social, emotional, and physical components of substance use and recovery. Experiencing an urge isn't a bad thing or an indication the user is doing something wrong. Consider it information. The important piece is what you do when you experience the trigger. The sooner the family and the user recognizes they're experiencing a trigger (usual response), the sooner they can use tools to manage the trigger (which we will discuss shortly). The longer someone stays in the trigger and debates their next choice (to use or not to use), the more likely they will give in to the urge.

How are triggers formed?

Triggers are formed by the memories we associate with an event. The brain avoids harmful situations (e.g., reminder of trauma, negative consequences of substance use) and reinforces positive ones such as highly pleasurable activities. These memories ensure we repeat that behavior or avoid it. When we're reminded of a situation, our brain signals the body to run away from the stimulus or go towards it. Our senses play a part in these memories. All sensory information (smells, sights, sounds) become associated with the event. As the brain prunes connections for efficiency, the sensory input becomes associated with the stimulus. It makes connections based on previous experience, whether or not it is directly connected.

A helpful way to better understand triggers is to discuss the "kindling effect." In some individuals, there is heightened response of the brain and body to an alcohol withdrawal episode. A person who goes through withdrawal symptoms when they stop drinking can experience a more intense withdrawal reaction in subsequent attempts to stop using. If that experience is repeated through a relapse, each episode (i.e., relapse, detox, return to use) intensifies the withdrawal and the negative associations. Although the specific reasons some people experience this are unknown, it is believed to be related to the neurochemistry of the brain. Prolonged exposure to substances alters brain chemistry. The effect is associated with increased neural excitability that "kindles" a more intense response. Each experience we have regarding triggers to use and withdrawal makes the next trigger even stronger. That pathway will be more accessible in the future. Repetition of the event will also add to the strength of that pathway. The stronger that connection becomes, the easier it is ignited.

Family Triggers

For families of substance users, the triggers will center around the user's actions. The families experience trauma around the user's actions, and fear responses develop. If the user is late coming home, that activates thoughts of past experiences where the abuser did not come home because of an all-night bender. Other events come to activate responses, such as a night out with friends, an unknown credit card charge, or the user's mood. These are all situations in which families experience triggers.

Family members aren't always able to predict their triggers until they experience them. Not all triggers are foreseeable. Some are common to substance using families. However, some are unique to each family. Predicting triggers is difficult because they are specific to their nervous system. Triggers can happen outside of our awareness and be related to a smell, a sound, a look, or any minute cue that a person's brain has associated with their loved one's using behavior. At times, they may not even be aware of their emotional response. Reactions to a stimulus or event don't have to be proportional to what's happening. For instance, a parent looks at their child's school grade book and sees an incomplete assignment. That triggers a response of anger and accusations of using drugs again. One missed assignment in most families would not cause this reaction. However, if a youth used drugs in the past and, as a result, failed classes, a parent's fear response would be activated from previous encounters.

When family members are triggered, they can have an intense response. The user may not have done anything wrong that they're aware of, in the present. The triggers can be internal, such as a feeling or a thought, or they can be external, like a smell, sound or sight.

Ironically, just as triggers are supposed to warn us of danger (at least, that's what our brain tells us), they can be counterproductive. They not only create stress and conflict but also further distance in families recovering from substances.

A family member and user may experience two different reactions to a trigger. A partner may feel uncomfortable with a former using friend dropping by the house unexpectedly, finding that threatening. Their trigger is also known as *traumatic coupling*. They associate this person—or, in some cases, event, object, or situation—with traumatic events (consequences of substance use). Loved ones can react strongly with fear, anger, suspicion, and sadness. Families have linked this person with events (the family member engaging in substance use with this person) in the past. The user views this differently. Feelings of excitement, euphoric recall of "good times" spent with their friend are, for them, a positive association. This coupling of a pleasurable experience and past use makes this visit from a friend a potential relapse trap for the user but may not be seen by the user as such.

It's helpful to recognize that triggers are normal. Nothing is wrong with either the family or user experiencing triggering situations. It's important for both parties to accept that triggers will occur. *The key is choosing our response to them.* For example, a user expresses a desire or thought to use substances, and they share it with you. A productive response is to view it as a vote of confidence that they chose to be honest with you and that this is an opportunity to build credibility with each other. Rather than acting on fear, choose to encourage the user and respond with gentle curiosity about how the user plans to negotiate that challenge. Navigating triggers are an expected part of recovery for all family members.

Examples of Internal and External Triggers

Internal Triggers	External Triggers
1. Come from within the person. 2. Result from a memory, an emotional response or something physical. 3. Are subjective and specific to the person.	1. Environmentally based. 2. Come from a person, place, event, or may be situationally activated.
Examples: A concert that comes to town can be a powerful trigger for a user if associated with a pleasurable using experience.	Examples: Returning to a physical location where substance use occurred in the past (e.g., a neighbor's yearly party, a favorite bar, a family event).
A weekend when using episodes typically occur.	A family member leaves on a trip and the user is left alone for the weekend.
An argument between family members. In the past, this type of event has triggered using.	Watching a television show/movie depicting a using event or situation.
A family member is in a bad mood. Substances are how they coped in the past. Previously, they would use to avoid dealing with the other person.	A time of day (e.g., after work, happy hour).
Experiencing a strong emotion. In the past, substances would have compensated for this emotion. It doesn't have to be related to a using situation.	An object associated with the recovering person's substance use (e.g., the user drinks from a cup formerly used for drinking, a specific lighter)
Feeling bored.	Running into a friend with whom they used in the past.

Despite the negative consequences associated with using substances, users often have difficulty resisting the urge to use again. The desire stems from the strong neurological, social, emotional, and physical components of substance use and recovery. Experiencing an urge isn't a bad thing or an indication the user is doing something wrong. The important piece is what they do when they experience the trigger. The sooner the family and the user recognize that they're experiencing a trigger (usual response), the sooner they can use tools to manage the trigger (which we will discuss shortly). The longer they stay in the trigger and debate their next choice (to use or not to use), the more likely they will give in to the urge.

Trigger Cycles

We have discussed how triggers are common for substance users as well as families. The longer we stay in the trigger, the greater the likelihood it will intensify. It becomes stronger if we stay in that trigger moment, regardless of how it came about. The trigger becomes a belief. Even though we recognize the trigger isn't healthy for us, its intensity overpowers our rational thought process. If we recognize the trigger and address it sooner, the intensity will lessen and eventually go away. If we give in to the trigger, we're only reinforcing it the next time we experience it.

The trigger cycle is where we spend more time debating the trigger and allowing it to become stronger. An example of a trigger cycle is if you're on a diet. You know eating chocolate cake isn't good for you. Instead of accepting the thought as true, *Maybe a few bites will be okay; one little break from my diet won't hurt*, you examine the thoughts and recognize this as a trigger.

The sooner we move to managing the trigger, the more likely we'll be to successfully work through it. Recognizing the trigger and moving to manage it is the ideal. We can then shift to problem-solving rather than entertaining the trigger.

Partly because of triggers, the user and family must be patient with the recovery process. It may take a while for the triggers to diminish in intensity. They create strong associations in the brain. Social, biological, neurological, and emotional factors are potent reinforcers of the pathway. It's helpful to make sure everyone knows that triggers are normal and we all must deal with them. Users cannot expect things to return to normal immediately when they stop using. Despite the consequences users experience with their use, they can still feel tempted to return to using. That urge doesn't go away with the decision to stop using substances. The user will continue to have their triggers to manage and navigate their way through.

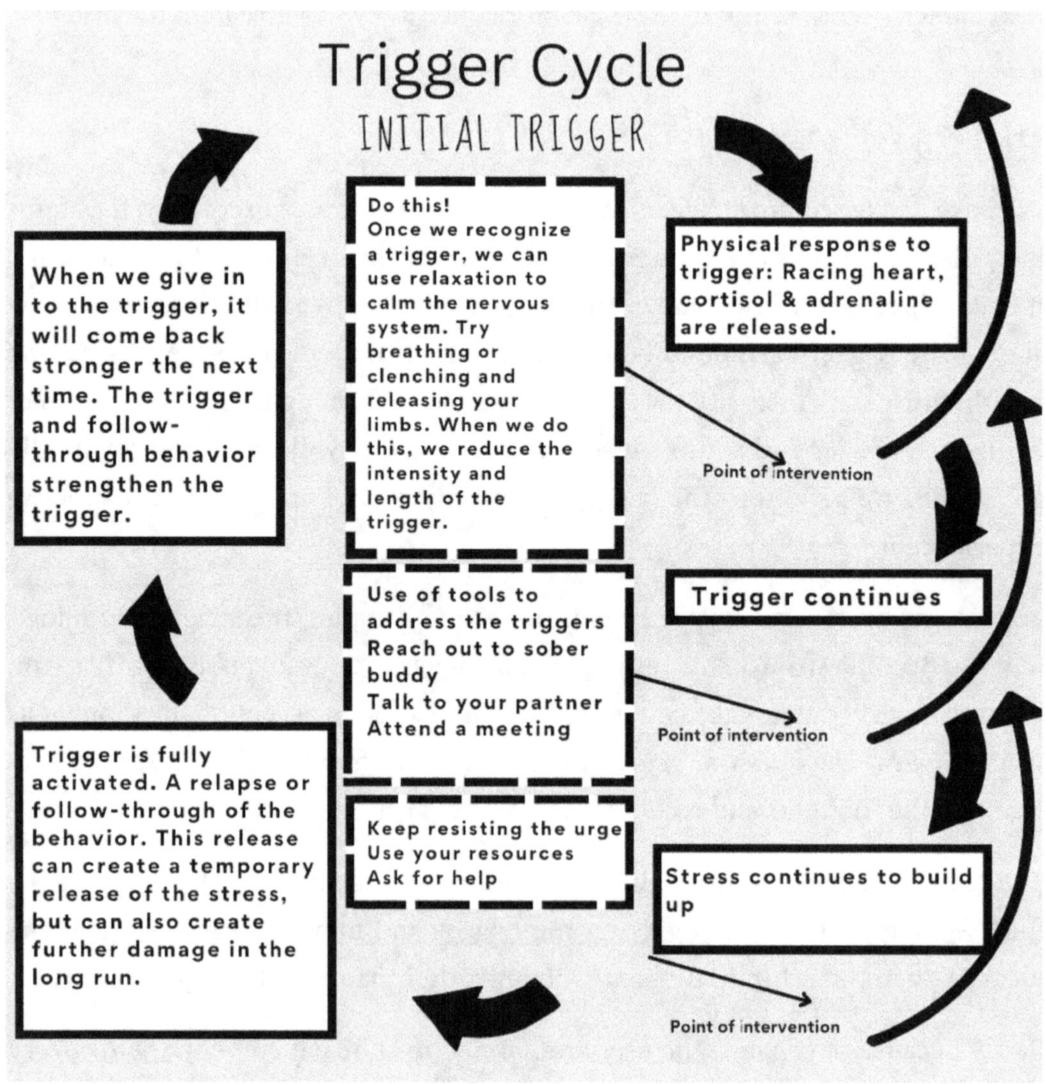

Family Trigger Exercise

The user's relationship with substance use will be different than that of family members. Family members will be feeling hurt, anger, and fearful of their loved one's return to substance use. There can be many reminders of the substance use they will have to navigate their way through, which elicit different feelings in the user. Family members' emotions will be coming from a different place.

It is helpful for families to repair the damage done by substance use to work on their communication. Their ability to be open and honest with each other has been damaged. Ideally, the user will be able to feel confident in sharing their triggers with their family. They will see loved ones as valuable allies in facing their challenges in recovery. Family members can also share their fears, concerns, and triggers openly.

The critical piece in families and users working together to repair the damage is trusting each other. Everyone needs to feel safe expressing their feelings, which will take time. The user will have to hear triggers from the family members. These triggers can create feelings of guilt and shame. For the family to listen to the user's trigger, they can experience feelings of anger and fear. The critical piece to this is creating an open dialogue.

Changing unhealthy communications will take time and preparation. It is helpful to predict and plan for triggers. Although we cannot always anticipate when a trigger will present itself, the more prepared we are, the more likely we will manage it successfully when it does arise.

Anticipating Triggers

We recommend that each family member completes their own worksheet:

Examples of Triggers	Response (What thoughts or emotions do you feel?)	What can I do to manage the triggers?	What will be helpful for my family to know? And how can they help?	What do I expect or need from my family?
Places				
People				

Events **(Dates, time** **of year, etc.)**				
Other				

. . . . . .

CHAPTER 7

Communicating About Triggers

. . . . . .

"Practicing gentle curiosity in response to triggers helps all parties to explore ways to understand one another and what drives their thoughts, feelings, and actions."

~Mark and Janet Myers

Trust takes time to rebuild, and triggers can be a significant roadblock in this process. Changing well-established communication patterns takes time as well. The user can significantly aid the recovery process through patience, understanding, and openness about what they're experiencing in their recovery and especially about the triggers they experience. The family will also need to be patient and productively expressive about their own triggers. In substance using families, secrecy and avoidance have been typical responses in the household. Trust and openness need time to develop. Practicing gentle curiosity in response to triggers helps all parties to explore ways to understand one another and what drives their thoughts, feelings, and actions.

The User and Family Communicate about Triggers

User	*Family*
Verbalize a Trigger Your family will eventually appreciate your openness and honesty. Let your family know when you see a potential trigger occurring. 1. You will have a recovery plan and need to use your tools. 2. Let the family in on your recovery plan and how you will address a trigger. This helps you mentally play out the plan and reassures your family. Win-win. 3. Remember, they may be as worried about the triggering event as you. 4. You are not on your own. Accept their assistance.	**Use Gentle Curiosity** It will be natural to experience fear when your family member discusses a trigger. Take a deep breath and instead be curious. 1. Ask about their recovery plan and tools. 2. Offer to assist. 3. Say, "Walk me through it." 4. Be encouraging. 5. Ask, "What will be the hardest part for you?" 6. "How can I help?" 7. Understand that it may be difficult for them to discuss their feelings and triggers. 8. Be patient.

Taking responsibility for regulating your emotions in the recovery process will help your partner and family to manage their emotions more effectively. It is expected that there will be intense emotions expressed throughout the recovery journey, but working on your own emotions and your ability to express them in a productive way allows all members of the family to grow.

User	*Family*
Manage your emotions: It's natural to experience strong emotions when beginning to discuss situations that have been secret for some time. Expect that your partner may receive this information with anger and sadness. It's important for the truth to be told, but go at a pace that suits the needs of everyone involved. 1. Identify what you're feeling. 2. Take breaks if emotions are running too high. Use that time to calm yourself. 3. Balance listening and talking. Alternate between listening intently and saying what's on your mind.	**Manage your emotions:** Strong emotions will be expressed in the process of recovery both on your part and the recovering person's part. If things have been kept from you, it's normal that you would experience anger and sadness. Be mindful of how these emotions are expressed, especially in early recovery. 1. Identify your own emotions. 2. Take breaks if needed. If one of you needs a break, you both need a break. Use that time to calm yourself. 3. Balance listening and talking. Alternate between listening intently and saying what's on your mind. 4. Remember, this process is for all of you. You have a dual role, helping the user and yourself.

Discussions about stopping substance use can be difficult conversations. It's helpful to approach them in a neutral fashion.

User	*Family*
Adopt an attitude of non-defensiveness: If we behave defensively, the conversation will take a wrong turn. Choose to look at the situation in the best terms possible. Tell yourself: 1. "My family wants my health and healing." 2. "We can heal as a family." 3. "They are not the enemy." State a concern without blaming others. This allows everyone to work on a situation together.	**Adopt an attitude of non-defensiveness:** When we attempt to communicate with someone about difficult topics, choose to see the best motives in the other person. 1. Listen to others without becoming defensive. 2. Your partner is not your enemy. 3. Say, "We can heal as a family." 4. State your concerns without blaming others. This allows you to be able to collaborate in recovery.

How we talk with one another sets the tone for conversations. Where, when, and the words we use can determine the productivity of conversations.

User	*Family*
Communicate your concerns: 1. At the right time – Avoid starting a conversation when you're impaired, tired, or already emotional. 2. Be aware of your tone, words, and gestures. These can be triggers. 3. Be honest – Remember secrecy, deception, and avoidance were what they saw when you were using. They'll have difficulty trusting you if they feel you're hiding things. 4. Save the snark – Sarcastic comments may feel satisfying, but they're not productive and will only derail the discussion. 5. Answer questions as you can, but it's okay to say that there are just some things you don't have answers to.	**Communicate your concerns:** 1. Be aware of your tone, words, and gestures. These can be triggers. If someone feels attacked, they'll hear less of what you say and focus instead on how you say it. When people feel attacked, a stress response is triggered, which will heighten the fight-flight-freeze response. 2. At the right time – The timing and setting of these conversations are so important. Make sure there will be enough time to finish a discussion. 3. Save the snark – Sarcastic comments may feel satisfying in the moment, but they're not productive and will only derail the discussion. 4. At times, you'll need to take leaps of faith that seem difficult. You can't keep the recovering person in a bubble. Let go of your need to control outcomes.

Intense emotion can make conversations difficult. Understanding what makes you (angry, frustrated, sad, fearful, etc.) will help make discussions more productive.

User	Family
Know your triggers: Each recovering person can identify and plan for the situations that are most likely to cause difficulties for them. Refer to the Trigger worksheet in the Tool section of this book.	**Know your triggers:** Families have their own triggers that need to be explored. Families can also work through their triggers with the Trigger worksheet.

Recovery is not just for the user. It's for all members of the family. Each one needs to care for their own needs and those of the children in recovery.

User	Family
Be responsible for your own recovery: Remember, you're responsible for your recovery. Your family will ask you to make and maintain commitments to avoid using. Respect for your family and your desire to remain sober will require that you work a recovery plan.	**Be responsible for your own recovery:** Remember, the responsibility of recovery lies with the recovering person. Frequently, family members feel responsible for the user's problems. You cannot control their decision-making and choices. Set clear and consistent boundaries for the user. You can choose to recover whatever the user chooses.

Family Recovery Strategies

- **Self-care** – Recovery can be a long road. Self-care also includes diet, exercise, sleep hygiene, and relaxation. Ensuring you care for your own well-being and that of family members allows you to be emotionally available to the tasks of recovery.

- **Support systems** – Support systems include family, friends, support groups, self-help groups, and professional help. Substance abuse families can feel isolated and lonely. It's beneficial to share your experiences in recovery. Similarly, allow yourself healthy breaks and diversion. Focusing exclusively on your loved one's substance use problems can be exhausting. Evaluate your support systems. Make sure you're getting what you need from them. Suppose you're working on reconciliation, and a family member is pushing you for divorce. In that case, this isn't the type of support you need. That doesn't mean you need to eliminate the person, but set limits to your discussions.

- **Spirituality** – A religious organization or institution that supports you and your family offers community and support for many individuals. Prayer, reflection, and meditation may be helpful components of your journey. Twelve-step programs also have this as a component.

- **Reality check** – If you find yourself emotionally charged, ask yourself some questions to clarify your feelings. Revisiting something that's happened in the past can be counterproductive. There may not be anything the user can do aside from listening and expressing their regret they've left you feeling this way. There is a delicate balance in focusing too much on processing the past. The goal is moving forward with respect for what has happened.

1. Is this feeling based on what has transpired in the past?

2. Are you responding to a situation that is currently happening?

3. Will discussing the situation be helpful?

4. What are you looking for from the user?

- **Mindfulness** – If you find yourself getting triggered frequently, consider using relaxation strategies and mindfulness techniques.

Imagine you're in a canoe on a calm lake. As you glide through the water, you experience thoughts and feelings that appear in your mind. Visualize that as the bow of the canoe slides through the water, you observe your thoughts and feelings fall to either side. Choose not to engage in the thoughts but let them fall to either side of the bow.

There are many apps, videos, and books that you can use to practice this skill. The more you practice, the easier it becomes to engage these skills when you really need them.

- **Practice empathy:** In most cases, the user will struggle with guilt about the circumstances. Continually reminding them of the problems they caused will not help in your recovery.

- **Be proactive:** You may not be able to predict all events and situations that will trigger you; however, there are some events you can anticipate. Discuss ways you can manage them and what the recovering person can do to reassure you. Again, there may not be something specific, but often the conversation will provide reassurance. We cannot avoid all circumstances that trigger us. However, some events may be too early in the recovery process to face. In those situations, avoidance may prevent backsliding.

- **Keep a journal:** Try a brain dump! Get your thoughts out of your head and onto paper and identify **your patterns of thinking and behaving.**

Rabbit Hole Thoughts

Overcoming triggers can involve dealing with rabbit hole thoughts. The term "rabbit hole" comes from a classic story called *Alice's Adventures in Wonderland* by Lewis Caroll. It refers to how anxious thoughts become unproductive. One question leads to another and yet another. Trying to produce an answer, or a preferred answer, winds up in a never-ending loop of possibilities, leading us down a tunnel into a dark hole. We get lost, feeling overwhelmed and frustrated, unable to resolve the issue by thinking about it. We keep revisiting the same thoughts that create the feelings. It can be difficult to find a way out. If we keep going over the same information, we can get stuck.

Thankfully, we can *recognize* that we're pursuing a rabbit hole thought, instead of entertaining the same thought over and over. What would happen if we invested our energy in getting through the moment and not in solving the problem? In that way, we can look for a way out of our rabbit hole thoughts. Eventually, it is possible to recognize the circumstances that lead to our rabbit holes and take evasive action.

Here's an example:

Situation: Jim went out on a first date with a woman from work. They appeared to have good chemistry, and he enjoyed the date. His rabbit hole thinking begins:

Did she have a good time?

I wonder how she'll act toward me at work on Monday.

Will work be awkward now?

What if this ends badly?

Jim continues to review the potential outcomes. Unfortunately, the way the future plays out is unknown. Despite his efforts, he really cannot find an answer now. The more effort he puts into getting answers, the more frustrating it will be for him.

Emotional response: Frustrated, anxious, annoyed, worried.

Coping thoughts: I'm not going to have an answer to this question. It's not productive for me to keep going over these questions.

What are my rabbit hole thoughts? _________________________________

____

____

____

What do I feel when I'm in my rabbit hole thoughts? _______________

____

____

____

How am I physically reacting to being in a rabbit hole? _______________

____

____

____

What will be my existing thought (what I tell myself to get out of this thinking)?

____

____

____

What interventions/strategies will I use when I am in these thoughts?

____

____

____

Recognizing that you're in a rabbit hole thought is helpful. The sooner you apply your energy to get out of these thoughts, the better you will feel.

Recovery is a Process, Not an Event

Once the use stops or the user makes a commitment to stop using substances, there will be much work that needs to be done by both parties. Overcoming the actual use is the first step. Managing triggers is part of the recovery process for all parties. As the process unfolds, the users and families can grow and learn much about each other.

The user must be patient with the family as they begin to understand and process their own triggers. In time, triggers fade—provided relapses don't reinforce them. There must be a balance between talking through triggers and recognizing that one must manage their own feelings. Avoidance of the topic will only strengthen the concerns of family members that there is something to hide. Overresponding will also create conflict. A continual state of confrontation is not helpful for anyone.

When a family experiences triggers, it will be more productive for the recovering user to acknowledge and not defend what is being expressed by a family member. The recovering partner has the challenge of feeling as if they must prove their innocence. To reassure family members and avoid this dilemma, we recommend using testing such as a breathalyzer or urinalysis. Not all families have the resources or time to verify sobriety. In most cases, if there are relapses, they will become evident over time. It's difficult to keep a relapse hidden for too long.

Reaction to a Significant Event

A physical and emotional response is created.

Our brain interprets and stores the event, and our response to it is encoded. We associate that event with either pleasurable or painful/dangerous.

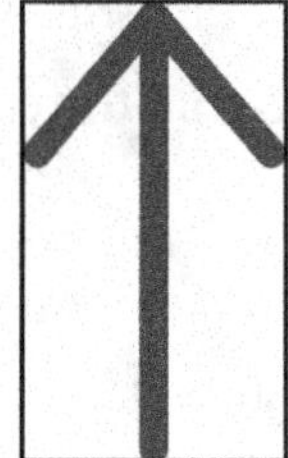

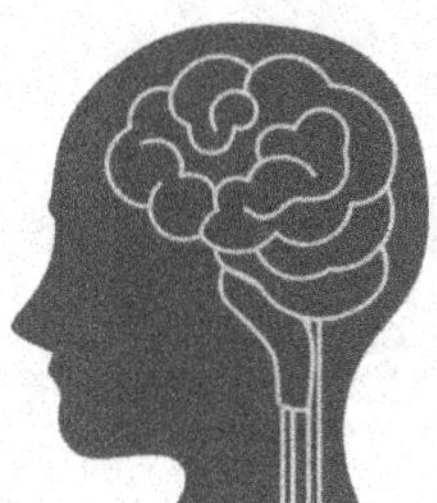

Anything we associate with the event will be factored into our next encounter. The actual event itself does not need to be exactly repeated for us to respond. The brain makes connections using sights, sounds, and other senses associated with that event.

Multiple factors influence our interpretation of an event, such as previous life experiences, personality, and the event itself.

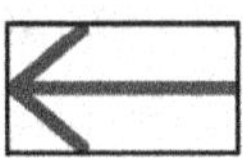

Notes for the Journey Home

Healing and trust take time to develop. The more planning and discussion that occurs, the more reassured families feel. We have included some additional suggestions:

- **Identify your triggers.** Learn to recognize the triggers that are unique to you. Once you can name the behaviors and emotions that trigger you, it will be possible to alter them.

- **Choose your response.** It's difficult to communicate when we're caught up in our emotions. Take time to calm yourself and understand what has triggered you. Once you understand, you're better able to respond instead of reacting to the trigger.

- **Share your triggers.** Once you understand your triggers, share them with your family so they can understand and respond in supportive ways. It's important to listen to one another and non-defensively respond.

- **Create an environment where it's safe to share your thoughts.** This may take time because of the damage done to relationships by substance use. To some extent, you must choose to start over. For the recovering user, being willing to hear how others have been hurt and what triggers occur are part of the process of establishing trust.

Each family has its own unique experiences as well as resources to draw upon. Other issues will pop up or become known when the use stops. If the focus is on the user, most attention will be on substance misuse. Other matters will get pushed to the background. In the initial stages of recovery, family and individual counseling will help families navigate the challenges they face and address issues that happened in the past.

CHAPTER 8

Changing Self-Talk

**"Each of you has growing to do. You will each accomplish
this goal at your own pace."**

~Janet and Mark Myers

Everyone has internal dialogue or self-talk to some degree. These are the things we say to ourselves subconsciously in our minds or even sometimes whisper aloud to ourselves. Our self-talk is based on our life experiences, our emotional state at the time, our perceptions about ourselves, our environment, and life stressors. It helps us process events and situations. In some cases, it could be positive. Used correctly, it can reduce stress, boost self-esteem, and improve sports performance, to name a few positive benefits.

Our internal dialogue can also take on a self-defeating or harmful tone. In these circumstances, our voice will be critical, negative, and self-defeating. The internal dialogue we're having with ourselves often may not even be realistic, and in most cases, it's not advice we would give to our friends. The longer the talk goes on, the more stress and negativity it creates. It is our own worst enemy.

In SUD families, self-talk plays a significant role. Family members can feel helpless when their loved one is struggling with a substance problem. They want so desperately to help them. They begin to try to control their loved one's use. Often, in trying to control the use and failing, they blame themselves. The user will latch onto this opportunity and will encourage these beliefs by family members. If the user can deflect blame onto another family member, they can continue their use. They are avoiding responsibility for their use as well as the consequences.

Adopt an Attitude of Non-defensiveness

Healthy discussions are a keystone to successful family recovery. The process of learning to communicate with one another in a healthy manner has been hampered by substance use for many years in most SUD families. We prevent effective communication by avoiding discussion, fearing confrontation, and deflecting the specter of blame. So often, we anticipate the accusation or the suggestion of blame that we react defensively before our family member utters a word.

Adopting an attitude of non-defensiveness offers family members a port in a storm. The family's own negative self-talk and self-limiting beliefs stand in the way of really listening to one another. Anticipating hearing criticism leads people to react defensively. Taking an approach of non-defensiveness helps to reduce the tension. "How do I do that?"

1. Breathe: Calm yourself first.

2. Be: Focus on the present.

3. Use "I" language: "I feel…, I think…, I need…" Stay away from statements starting with "You," as in, "You did this…"

4. Choose to respond vs. react: Stay on topic. It's okay to plan some responses ahead of time.

Be Compassionate

As individuals and families begin to heal from substance use disorder, they must contend with a variety of emotions that may drive their behavior. Shame is a complicated emotion that requires radical compassion to combat. Learning to challenge the negative thinking and emotions involved in shame will require all family members to respond to one another in a compassionate manner.

Recognize the Path

Taking this journey in family recovery leads us on a path of discovery that changes the known trajectory of our lives and relationships. We must look at our patterns, both positive and negative. It requires honesty and transparency. Telling the truth about the patterns we have created to sustain substance use involves all family members. This concept is often difficult for the non-user to process. Each of you has growing to do. You will each accomplish this goal at your own pace.

Find Your Voice

In substance use disorder families, a greater effort is typically invested in the family trying to stop their loved one's use than the loved one is putting into stopping. Families become frustrated. Often members blame themselves for their loved one's use. The user will even promote this thought. As a result, unhealthy ways of thinking are developed by the family. The longer this type of thinking continues, the more likely the thoughts become engrained.

Self-Talk Worksheet For Family Members		
Type of Thinking	**Negative Self-talk**	**Positive Self-talk**
If only	"If only they could understand how bad the use is." "If only their job wasn't as stressful."	"They're responsible for their decisions." "They've been told how problematic their use is but choose not to listen."
Maybe	"Maybe the use isn't so bad." "Maybe I'm overreacting."	"My loved one's use is a problem." "We've talked about it numerous times." "The problem of the use has been discussed before."
Time location	"If we move, they'll stop using." "After the holidays, it'll get better."	"My loved one's use is not dependent on dates or time. "The use has been a problem regardless of when or where."
My fault	"I'm causing my loved one to use." "I stress out my loved one and that's why they choose to use."	"My loved one is responsible for the use." "I can't cause or make someone use."
I could stop this	"I have to do something to stop my loved one's use."	"I can't control their decisions." "I only control my decisions." "My loved one chooses to use."
I'm stuck	"I have no choice but to stay in this situation."	"There are always choices." "All the options may not be great, but we can still make choices, even if these choices are how we manage moments."
Try Harder	"I need to try harder to understand my loved one."	"Just because a person isn't doing what I want them to do doesn't mean I'm not trying." It just means they're not listening."
Just listen to me	"I need to keep trying to get my loved one to listen." "If they listened to me, then they would understand."	"My loved one may hear what I'm saying but chooses not to listen. It means they're choosing not to change and not wanting to hear what I have to say."

Reversing a Shame Spiral

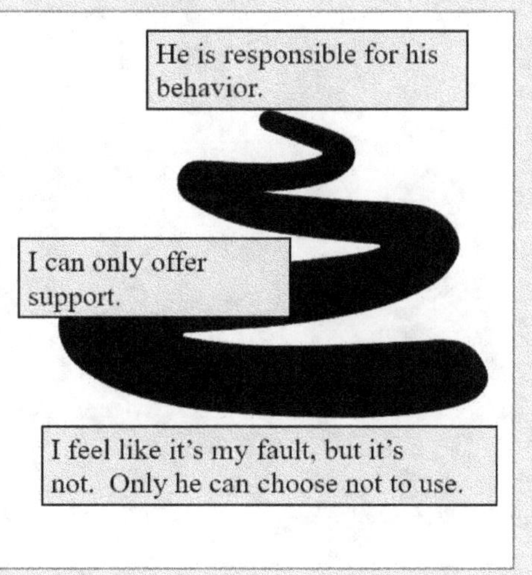

1. **Identify the negative self-perceptions in your shame spiral.**

   Add an example in each box.

2. **Use your examples to develop "challenge" thoughts to reverse your spiral.**

   These are reality-based positive or neutral thoughts that help us to reverse the self-destructiveness of shame.

CHAPTER 9

Reestablishing Roles

**"Family member(s) can choose recovery even if
the user decides to continue using."**

~Mark Myers and Janet Myers

As part of the recovery process, each family member must renegotiate their role in the family. Each one must adapt to substance use in their life. When substances are removed from their lives, it changes how everyone in the family interacts. This adjustment creates significant conflict within the family. Regardless of the difficulties faced within the family on their journey, it's important to understand that family members can choose recovery even if the user decides to continue using.

Family Fallout

One of the realities of substance use disorder is the fallout that occurs within the family. Children and partners experience erratic and unpredictable behavior that dramatically affects them. This developmental type of trauma occurs over time. It makes individual family members feel helpless and unable to effect change in their lives. Recovery for family members requires that we develop an understanding of the impact of these experiences.

Anger, fear, and disbelief are the first emotions families experience when a family member begins to recover. The individual may start by giving up substances, but much more must happen. While they focus on their recovery journey and making the right choices, the family must find their way as well. The recovering person can seem very self-involved, and, to some extent, they need to be. However, the family doesn't know how to process the changes. This season can be tremendously difficult and unsettling.

Staying in the relationship or leaving is often a consideration. Families must balance the potential benefits and challenges. While the user in recovery learns to replace using behaviors, the family must adjust to the changes occurring within the recovering person. They each must develop new routines and healthy habits of their own. Discussing and negotiating how these new routines and habits occur is the task of the family in recovery.

The partner or spouse of the recovering user has likely been on their own in raising children, completing household responsibilities, and maintaining the status quo for the recovering person. There is significant hurt and resentment to address through therapy for all involved parties.

Adapting Family Roles

In the using family, members learn to be either self-reliant or overly dependent. Often, there does not seem to be a middle ground.

Those children who've learned to be self-reliant are often unwilling to accept attempts by the individual in recovery to reassert authority as a parent. These roles absolve the substance user from responsibility for their using behavior. The user can feel left out and isolated. This isolation can prevent the user from seeking and receiving the help they need.

The user's behavior is unpredictable, and their children may struggle, at times, to be vulnerable or transparent due to the risks of their unpredictable environment. The experiences in SUD families lead to interactional patterns that can make later-life relationships more difficult. They can be hypervigilant, distrustful, and have difficulty regulating their emotions. Some may become numb to their feelings and those of others. Those children who've learned to be self-reliant are often unwilling to accept attempts by the individual in recovery to reassert authority as a parent. These roles absolve the substance user from responsibility for their using behavior. It can prevent the user from seeking and receiving the help they need. In addition, there are long- and short-term consequences that deplete the integrity of the family unit, including emotional, physical, and mental health. Substance use disorder becomes all-consuming and ultimately destructive to one's most personal relationships, especially with family members.

Six Common Family Roles of the SUD Family

Substances change the way one thinks and behaves, causing the family to think and behave differently in support or alternately in reaction to the substance user. These changes cause family members to begin to fill certain roles within the family, of which six have been commonly identified. These include: the substance user, the hero, the caretaker, the scapegoat, the mascot, and the lost child. Although not every family member aligns with these roles and often roles overlap, it can be a helpful framework to understand the way family members respond in a substance use disordered family (16).

The Hero

The hero's role is to be the public face of the family. The hero appears super-responsible, independent, high achieving, perfectionistic, and tends to hide their emotional or mental distress. Behind the scenes, they engage in "fixing" behaviors such as getting rid of substances, putting the substance user to bed, and literally and figuratively cleaning up after the substance user.

The Caretaker

Caretakers can be similar or overlap with heroes. This role has also been called the "enabler" or "martyr," exhibiting behaviors that support the status quo such as covering for the substance user, lying, maintaining the happy family image, and sacrificing their needs for the substance user's. This role is often characterized by denial.

Fixers such as heroes and caretakers often find themselves repeating these patterns in adulthood. These individuals tend to please and appease others. Developed in traumatic and unpredictable environments, they learn to agree and make things pleasant to please others. The accommodation helps for the moment, but not in the long run. As they become adults, this pattern can be toxic in relationships. The coping patterns of pleasing and appeasing, developed to help the child deal with the stress of their home, no longer serve the individual in present relationships.

Self-care is an important skill to learn when recovering as a fixer. It can be a challenge to let go of the role because it offers the illusion of control in what used to be an uncontrollable situation. When the family begins to recover, caring for yourself becomes your priority. This may initially be uncomfortable for fixers. Focus on being present in your life and be conscious of where you put your attention and energy.

The Scapegoat

The person in the role of scapegoat diverts attention away from the substance abuser. They may act out in response to their tendency to be isolated and blamed for the problems in the family. These individuals often carry shame for the family. They are more likely to become substance abusers themselves and have difficulties in relationships with other family members and their intimate relationships as an adult. In addition, the scapegoat has an awareness of the true issues in the family and tries to call attention to the problems.

Challenging the narrative imposed by the family and fighting back empowers the scapegoated individual to harness their resilience and become healthy. While the family may have coped by blaming you for the family's problems, you have a choice of how you will live. Learning healthy coping skills is extremely important as part of the recovery process for the person in this role.

The Mascot

The mascot keeps things pleasant and uses humor to distract from the more painful aspects of the substance use. They may see the seriousness of the problem but feel helpless to change or impact the situation. They may have difficulty recognizing the pain they experience in the substance using family and may struggle with anxiety or depression.

The Lost Child

Lost children behave in contrast to the chaos in the family. They stay out of sight and avoid conflict. Their role allows the rest of the family to focus on the substance user. These individuals develop issues with assertiveness and self-worth.

Mascots and lost children often feel invalidated within the family and develop a sense of learned helplessness in relationships. When family members deny their own emotional pain, they can become anxious and depressed. It's important that they recognize the impact substance use is having in their life. They must learn healthy coping skills for recovery.

Developing healthy roles within the family requires each member of the family to recognize how substance use has, individually and as a family, impacted them. A good start is creating an environment where the family can openly discuss substance use and how they've been affected. When the family navigates new roles in a healthy manner, home becomes more predictable and safer for all family members.

Sibling Relationships

Substance use problems extend beyond the user. Fights, verbal and physical, legal issues, work problems, broken promises, and numerous other events or situations are common in substance-abusing families. Those are the apparent effects that SUD has on families. However, in most cases, the damage goes beyond what we see on the surface. Children are particularly vulnerable to the consequences of substance use, especially when a sibling is abusing substances.

Sibling relationships play an essential role in family life. These relationships are typically longer than any other relationship a person experiences over their lifetime. We learn a great deal from having a sibling. In most cases, siblings are the first peer relations we will have. Sibling relationships teach social skills, problem-solving skills, and how to resolve conflict. Other benefits include companionship, reality testing, guidance, role modeling, and support. Studies have identified that healthy sibling relationships benefit individuals in later life. Positive family relations significantly impact children's overall development (18).

Substance use in the family creates significant stress in sibling relationships for several reasons. When children fulfill the roles of hero, scapegoat, caretaker, user, mascot, or lost child, they may experience patterns of interaction that complicate and cause conflict between family members and may pit siblings against one another. The children lose out not only on the benefits of a sibling relationship (listed above), but also on their parent relationships. As a result, they experience the following emotional challenges:

- A sense of loneliness or lack of connectivity

- Difficulties making decisions for fear of drawing attention to themselves

- Feeling rejected

- Encountering depression

- A lack of confidence

- Distorted sense of family

- Deficits in social skills and problem-solving. They will not have parental or sibling guidance to give feedback and help them navigate social situations.

- Resentment and anger toward using child

- Sense of obligation

Sibling birth order factors into substance using families. Older children tend to take on more responsibilities in families as a rule. If the older child is a substance user, the younger sibling experiences either a lack of a role model or negative role modeling. Younger children in substance-using families also take on more responsibilities usually designated to the older child or parents. These situations lead to an imbalanced family structure and role assignment. If a younger sibling is the user, the older child tends to feel responsible for taking care of the family's needs and being well-behaved. This leaves the older sibling with an intense feeling of shame and guilt.

Children feel discouraged even if the family is open about the substance abuse. They feel frustrated that the problem isn't getting fixed. The more prolonged and problematic the use, the more disheartening the experience for the other children.

Each family member goes through the unique challenges associated with a substance-using family. Siblings often get lost in these families, and it's helpful for parents to be aware of this dynamic. It's essential to be mindful of all family members, especially the ones who are not drawing attention.

Family Routines Worksheet

Routines are important for families. They provide structure and predictability that are important for everyone. For adults, routines offer healthy habits and reduce stress. For children, direction, a sense of belonging, feeling safe, and guidance are among the benefits they receive. Rituals may be as simple as having breakfast together, reading at bedtime, or having a family night. It's a way for families to reconnect and bond in community.

In families that experience a substance use disorder, routines become disrupted. The substance of choice takes over. The loss of routine increases the stress they experience. In recovery, it's helpful to reestablish previous routines as well as establishing new, healthier ones.

Helpful tips for reestablishing positive routine and creating new healthy family rituals:

- **Take a family survey. Each person should answer the following questions:**

  What routines do I share in the family? What do I like about them?

  What could I do to help with this routine?

  What are some routines I like? What do I like about them?

  What are some routines I don't like? Why don't I like them?

  What gets in the way for us as a family to getting things done?

- **Start small:** Build on your success. Small changes over time have a big impact.

- **Identify barriers** that would make these routines more difficult to complete. These barriers could be financial, time, energy, or habits. Make the goals realistic.

- **Be patient:** It could take some time to reestablish routines and create new ones.

- **Allow time for feedback from all family members.** Their feedback is necessary to ensure the success of the routines.

- **Plan:** Structuring your time makes it more likely for the event to take place.

- **Be flexible:** A parent's idea of a routine will be different than a youth's idea. Parents and kids operate from different value systems and perspectives. For a parent, it's helpful to be flexible. However, routines and rituals still need to be evaluated by parents to determine how they will fit into the rhythm of family life.

- **Do a two-week check-in:** Now that you've given it some time, let's check in and evaluate your progress. We understand that two weeks will only give us a small sample of progress and challenges. However, getting all family members' feedback ensures we continue with our successes and continue to work on our challenges.

- **Follow-up survey for each family member:**

  How would you evaluate how the two weeks went?

  What was helpful?

  What did you find difficult?

  What suggestions would you make to improve or build on the reestablishing of routines? How did family members help?

  What could they improve (constructive feedback only)?

Notes for the Journey Home

Here are some helpful strategies for reestablishing family roles:

- **Acknowledge there's a problem if you're a parent.** Don't be ashamed or embarrassed that substance use exists in the family.

- **Keep family activities and routines intact when possible.** Consistency helps children cope with family change. SUD families tend to isolate themselves. Encouraging children to participate in activities outside the home—whether that's sports, clubs, or religious groups—is healthy for them and helps them feel connected to other resources.

- **Check in with all family members.** These discussions are essential for quiet family members who may feel relegated to the background. Spend individual time with children and your partner.

- **Validate their frustrations.** It's okay for them to feel angry and disappointed. These situations take time to heal.

- **Be realistic.** It's okay to say, "I don't know." Don't make excuses for the user. Prepare your child; there will be some ups and downs.

- **Educate your child about addiction.** That information will be helpful and empowering.

- **Monitor grades and reach out to teachers or schools.** They can be tremendous resources for your child. Some schools may even have groups your child can attend.

- **Explore individual counseling for non-using children.** Their therapist can be both a sounding board and an advocate for them.

Each family uniquely experiences SUD. The same applies to individual family members. Siblings experience or interpret home events from their own perspectives. Families are resilient and draw upon their strengths. Recognizing the needs of all family members in the process of treating the SUD family allows hope for health and healing.

· · · · · · ·

CHAPTER 10

Family Communication and Building Trust

· · · · · ·

"Shame tends to grow in darkness and secrecy."

~Janet and Mark Myers

Communication presents a challenge in many recovering families. Talking with family members about substance use and its impact on the family can be difficult. Often, secrets have been a significant factor in substance use, and finding ways to discuss both the use history and the recovery needs to be brought into the open. Continuing to keep secrets reinforces the secrecy and shame that flourish during substance use. Shame grows in the dark.

Shame

Shame is believed to originate from an ancient word meaning "to cover." It's a painful feeling arising from one's own negative self-evaluation and the fear of that being exposed. SUD families fear that the use will continue, that they'll lose their family unit, and that they'll lose family members. The user fears, *If my family knew the truth, they would leave or hate me. My family will see me as weak because I used.* Feeling ashamed prevents them from bringing the secrets into the light.

Shame is different for everyone within the family. People take responsibility for situations that are not their fault. Internalizing this sense of shame and guilt prevents loved ones from seeing the reality of their situation. Although events happen within the family that may not be acceptable from an objective point of view, families do need to contend with the real-life circumstances that occur. Your family's reality will be unique.

You may ask, "Why do family members feel shame?" It's not rational, and it's part of the illness of substance use disorder. People who encounter substance use end up feeling shame for their part in the circle. This tends to lead to more destructive behaviors for the substance user and potentially codependent behaviors for the family. Shame is a common component of addiction. The thoughts and beliefs involved in shame reinforce self-loathing and prevent the individual from accepting their worth and dignity as a human being.

Shame tends to grow in darkness and secrecy. It whispers and sometimes shouts that we are unworthy of respect, love, or dignity. Whether it's the substance user or the family member, it impacts everyone, and the only way to address it is to "make the unknown… known." Keeping it hidden only perpetuates the circumstances that feed the disease.

When you talk about shame and fear, you demystify it. You take it from the shadows and allow others to help and care for you. The other thing is that talking about shameful feelings and thoughts allows family members to know, process, repair, rebuild trust, and eventually move on from the damage caused by substance use. We also discover that others share the same feelings and struggles we do, and that can reduce shame's impact on us; we are not alone in our shame.

Dealing with Resentment

So, how do families in recovery communicate when it has been so difficult? It's tempting to avoid complex topics and treat them as no longer relevant when sobriety begins; however, this isn't the most productive approach. A great deal of healing happens when families speak about their experiences. Fear tends to keep family members and the recovering person from exploring the substance use history and the impact on one another. Putting words to their situation is the beginning of healing.

Resentment is a hurdle SUD family members must negotiate. Especially when the use has gone on for a long time, and there have been many "attempts" at recovery, family members create a kind of brick wall around themselves to prevent the hurt and disappointment from the continued use. However, it doesn't stop them from experiencing hurt, and it eliminates the ability to communicate with the recovering user.

Notes for the Journey Home

Here are some guidelines for addressing the resentments, secrets, and shame that have occurred in the family trying to recover from substance use disorder:

- **Make the unknown known.** Often, the most significant anxiety, depression, and shame come from situations we've attempted to hide or that we've feared. The outcome may not always be what we hope. However, discussing the situation creates knowledge, and knowledge is power.

- **Take control of the things you can!** You can't control others, what others say, what others do, or their journey. You can control what you think, feel, and act in any situation. Recognizing what is within your control is vital to the recovery journey.

- **RESPOND vs. REACT.** Often, on the recovery journey, we feel we're reacting to circumstances outside of our control. Choosing our response to the substance user and the circumstance within that journey gives you a measure of control. It allows you to conserve your energy for important situations.

- **Is this a hill I choose to die on?** We must save our more significant fights for those that are most meaningful to us. If we battle with the substance user over every little thing, we exhaust ourselves. If we fight with the individual over every aspect of their recovery, our words lose their impact.

- **Extend grace.** Families spend so much time focused on what has gone awry during recovery. Each family member needs to give themself a break. Be kind, patient, and compassionate to one another.

- **Collect coping skills.** Strategies such as mindfulness, relaxation, and reframing can help rewire the brain's neurobiology for the user and family members. Despite the decisions made by the substance user, families can recover by attending to their own needs.

- **Self-care.** Caring for your health and well-being through healthy eating habits, exercise, sleep, and time with friends and family who support you creates health within the family.

When the family learns to address the various levels of shame that have developed among the members, recognize their shame triggers, and cope effectively with new paths both in the brain and in the life of the family, they make home a healthier, more comfortable place to be.

Self-Care

Healing from substance use disorder has implications for all family members. Each person in the family needs to be concerned with caring for themselves as well. In some families, the user has had the focus and attention. To heal, each family member must evaluate their own needs and seek balance. We recommend using this information to journal about some of your self-care habits. The following are some areas to consider:

✓ Relaxation: Learning to relax and breathe effectively lowers stress hormones such as cortisol and reduces anxiety. How do you relax?

✓ **Healthy eating**: Eating foods rich in Omega 3 fatty acids can improve mood. **Are there changes that need to be made to your eating habits?**

✓ **Hydration**: Drinking enough water is essential for well-being. Even minor dehydration can mimic symptoms of depression. Eight glasses a day is a reasonable goal. **Do you consume enough water?**

✓ **Exercise**: Regular physical activity is an excellent outlet for stress and can be as effective as antidepressants in reducing symptoms of depression and anxiety. **What type of exercise would fit your lifestyle?**

✓ **Sleep**: Adequate sleep improves mood and health, allows for consolidation of memory, and promotes repair of every system in the body. **How much sleep do you get each night?**

✓ **Leisure activities**: The ability to have fun is underrated. Everyone needs to recharge their batteries and enjoy life. **What is fun for you?**

✓ **Meaningful work**: Engaging in work that feels meaningful contributes to better mental health and a sense of purpose. **Do you find your work to be meaningful? Why or why not?**

✓ **Education**: Whether it's attending college, pursuing an advanced degree, or reading books, stimulating your mind improves mental health. **Do you feel as if you engage in continuous self-improvement? What would that look like for you if you did?**

✓ **Support system**: Making connections with peers, colleagues, family members, and supportive people allows us to feel less alone. **Identify your support system.**

✓ **Attitude**: Your mindset matters. Daily focusing on positive self-talk allows us to view the world in new ways. **How is your attitude?**

Self-Compassion

Self-compassion is fearlessly recognizing we are, all of us, flawed human beings and consciously choosing to accept kindness from ourselves and others. In families that cope with SUD, shame often interferes with many aspects of accepting self-compassion.

There are three interactive parts to self-compassion:

1. **Self-kindness:** Be gentle and empathetic with yourself.

2. **Mindful attention:** Recognize your thoughts, feelings, and behaviors. Learn to observe but not engage with them.

3. **Common humanity:** All humans fail and fall short of ideal.

Our ability to recognize and be compassionate with ourselves through the process of recovery enables us to look fearlessly at the places in our lives that need changing. It provides us with the discernment to know what someone else's issue is and what is our own. Telling ourselves the truth about our role in recovery helps all family members and frees us from the guilt and shame we've accumulated through our loved one's addiction.

Self-Compassion Worksheet

This following worksheet is based on the work of Dr. Kristine Neff. She defines self-compassion as learning to be kind to ourselves while mindfully being curious about our thoughts, feelings, and behaviors. Recognizing and responding gently to our humanity allows us to respond gently with others. The purpose of this worksheet is to learn to apply the idea of being kind and compassionate with ourselves to the process of recovery.

The first row is a common example of a response to a situation and how we can use self-compassion to think and feel differently about our role in recovery. You can use the blank rows to fill in details specific to your situation to help you use self-compassion to think and respond differently.

Situation	Self-Kindness	Mindfulness	Common Humanity
Your partner drinks and you have a horrible argument. He storms off and you fear a relapse is imminent.	Remind yourself you cannot make another person drink. Kindly and gently reassure yourself that you are okay.	Calm your mind. Observe your thoughts, but do not engage with them. Allow yourself to relax.	It's human to be angry at times. The emotion of anger is okay. Conflict happens. Identify your part.

Kristin Neff, PhD. *Self-Compassion: The Proven Power of Being Kind to Yourself.* Harper Collins, New York, NY, 2011 (19).

. . . . . .

CHAPTER 11

Parenting a Child with a Substance Use Disorder

. . . . . .

**"It's the middle part of that journey that is most challenging,
but there is a way through with support."**

~Mark and Janet Myers

At this point, we want to offer more specific information on a parent's role with a substance-abusing child. Addressing a child's substance use is not always clear. On the one hand, you can't control their decision-making. As much as parents would like to believe they can get their kids to do what they want, they can't. Parents can influence, direct, support, and guide their children, but ultimately it's their child's decision. Kids make mistakes and bad choices. Parents can't protect them from their decision-making. The older the child, the less influence parents have over their children's choices. This isn't easy to accept for most parents. The potential consequences of drug or alcohol use make it scary for parents.

Most parents instinctively feel accountable for their children's actions and decisions. If their child misbehaves in class and the teacher sends a note home, a parent may feel judged. Their perception is not necessarily reality. They may feel guilty or believe they did something wrong as a parent. Parents do feel responsible for what their child has done. These feelings aren't necessarily a logical conclusion but a common reaction from parents.

What to Look For

It's easier for some parents to pretend the problem isn't there. There are many reasons behind this, including lack of awareness, indifference from a parent, or the parent has their own challenges. The warning signs of youth substance use include:

Mood changes, especially irritability

- Academic problems

- Changes in appearance

- Changes in peer group

- Changes in eating and sleeping habits

- Decrease in social activities

- Behavior problems in school, home, or the community

- More argumentative, challenging authority

- Poor decision-making

- Substance use paraphernalia (pipes, empty bottles of alcohol, vapes, glass tubes)

If a parent checks off several of these, it doesn't necessarily mean the youth is using substances. Some of these are indicators of other concerns, such as a mental health issue or maybe a sign your teen is acting like a teen. The warning signs are red flags that warrant further investigation.

The challenging part in addressing substance use with the young population results from the fact that the consequences are less impactful to them than they would be for an adult. A job loss is more difficult for an adult than a youth. It's the same thing with a drop in grades or even family relationships. Developmentally, they're not as mature, and their brains need to be fully developed to have the same insight into potential risks as an adult. Therefore, in most cases, there will be a different level of investment in stopping for young people than for adults. The challenge is in getting an adolescent to buy into stopping their use.

Commitment to Sobriety

There are three possibilities a parent will face when it comes to identifying teen substance use.

1. There's a clear indication they're using substances and they're not invested in altering their use. They don't want to stop. They're resistant, defiant, and combative when it comes to discussing them stopping.

2. The child and the parent acknowledge the teen's use is a problem and they want to quit. There is a commitment to eliminating substance use. The focus is now on *how* to stop, not *if* they should stop using substances.

3. The teen is ambivalent about stopping. Their commitment to quit vacillates.

Developmentally, adults and teens are obviously at different points in their lives. It's not productive for parents to spend time trying to convince their teenage children the value of remaining alcohol- and drug-free. Since their life experiences are much more limited than adults', that value proposition will be less meaningful to them. The seriousness of drug or alcohol involvement will be limited to what they see in school, on social media, and what they know from their lives. They'll see using less concerning for them than for their parents. A substance-abusing youth who has no investment in stopping their use will need the motivation to come from the outside (externally) of them, such as a parent, school, coach, or probation officer, instead of a personal buy-in (internally) to quit using.

It's vital for the parent to avoid overexplaining or trying to reach a child to accept the merits of stopping their use. Most teens in this position won't be convinced their use is problematic. A parent's investment should focus more on their response to the use or consequences that will happen if they decide to continue. In this situation, a parent's role is to **raise a youth's discomfort level** regarding their use, such as limiting their access to friends, taking away their phone, disabling internet access. If their use is creating discomfort, their motivation to stop will hopefully increase. We have talked about how, by nature, humans seek pleasure and avoid pain or discomfort. At this age, a teen would not buy into future consequences such as health risks as much as an adult. They're focused, for the most part, on the here and now. What would entice the young person to change? Making the here and now uncomfortable enough for them is often a catalyst that leads the young person to change.

It's essential to recognize that youth have more information at their disposal than their parents did growing up. More information, however, doesn't mean accurate. An example is marijuana, which has become legal in many states in the US. The medical benefits of marijuana have been highly touted. However, the Federal Drug Administration has approved only a handful of medical conditions for treatment with marijuana. Some conditions have been the subject of limited research. However, if someone is searching the internet, they would find information that would indicate support for the use of marijuana for many health concerns. Sometimes, the results are based on poor research conditions (i.e., low sample size, faulty data collection) or self-report rather than scientific evidence. The adolescent won't look at information they gather with a critical eye. They'll more readily use the information that supports their pleasure-seeking activity of using. It is also significant to note that during adolescence, brain development activity is at its highest since early childhood.

It is helpful to have direct conversations with your child regarding substance use. That's a healthy dynamic in families. However, be mindful of nonproductive discussions. Informing a child about the problems associated with drugs will have limited results. The child is more interested in convincing you it's okay for them to use and will invest time and energy to that end. "That'll never happen to me," "It's not like that," or "According to Marijuana Forever (this is a made-up publication just to illustrate a point), marijuana's good for you" are topics you'll likely hear from your child. Parents will find themselves fact-checking and arguing with the adolescent about using substances. Energy is better spent, in this case, focusing on getting them to stop rather than convincing them they shouldn't use drugs.

For example, a three-year-old child walks up to a parent right before dinner and asks if they could have a big piece of chocolate cake. Most parents would say no. Three-year-olds do not like that answer and will try again to convince the parents that they could both finish all their dinner AND have cake, if they could have cake now. The longer the debate, the more invested and insistent the child becomes about having that cake. The longer we spend debating with the child or attempting to convince them they don't need cake right now, the less productive the interaction becomes. A firm and clear NO at the first request will shift that child into productive problem-solving. They could have something healthy to eat instead, distract themselves, or look for other ways to manage their hunger. They don't need to continue to go over why they shouldn't have the cake. Focusing on WHAT to do when they're hungry and must wait for dinner is a more productive discussion.

Parent-Child Communication Strategies

Ultimately, the decision to use is up to your child. Parents provide obstacles and consequences to their use. For teens to stop their use, the consequences of using substances must outweigh their perceived benefits. It's helpful to keep the following ideas in mind:

- **Enforce consequences.** Remember, your child is choosing to continue to use and receive the result of their choices. It's important to recognize this when you're implementing the consequences. It will be more productive if conversations are directed toward their choice to use substances and not defending why you're providing consequences. If you're ambivalent and sporadic in enforcing consequences, this will be confusing and ineffective for the teen.

- **Avoid getting into arguments.** Arguments are unproductive and steer families away from meaningful discussions, such as finding out why substances are so vital to them. Or why would they continue to use despite the consequences?

- **Try not to lecture, preach, or scold.** Instead, offer encouragement such as "I know you can do this" or "I know this will be hard for you, but I have confidence you can do it." Parents should steer conversations toward their inability to stop using or decision to keep using substances despite consequences.

- **Monitor your own substance use.** Remember, you're a role model and trying to convey a message. That message becomes ineffective if you're abusing substances yourself.

- **Present a united front in the message you give your children.** This isn't a time to play good parent/bad parent. The message will be more effective if they hear the same thing from both parents. All family members should be on board and be transparent in their concerns about the youth's using substances.

- **Praise positive choices when you see them.** Engage in healthy interactions like positive reinforcement of good behavior other than discussions of the use. Work together toward building new lifestyle patterns (e.g., work out together, walk, or start an eating plan together).

- **Be patient if their use isn't a life-threatening situation.** It may take a while for your message to sink in with them.

- **Develop your support systems.** Identify the strengths of your support systems and use them accordingly. Turning to a person for advice will be different than talking with someone who's a good listener.

For a child who recognizes they have a use problem, their motivation to stop is higher. This will be a more productive conversation than you'd have with a youth who refuses to give up their substance use. Consequences are still a factor, but the talks focus on how to stop using versus whether they should. Discoveries or admissions of use are more indicative of something going wrong in their recovery plan versus just deciding to use substances.

In previous chapters, we covered the difficulties in stopping, even with a solid commitment to abstain. Many factors make quitting a challenging task. The beginning part of the journey is committing to stop. Once they're grounded in their recovery, their life will start improving. That is the end goal of the journey. It's the middle part of that journey that is most challenging, but there is a way through with support.

Notes for the Journey Home

There are essential points to remember in this journey. First, your child's recovery is going to be their path. You cannot put yourself in the position of having all the answers. A parent's role is to assist, support, and encourage their path. The youth need to put in the work to make it happen. That concept goes against most parents' instincts. Parents don't want to see their children go through pain. They must resist these inclinations and allow their children to drive their own recovery. This may mean your child loses friends or must change their peer group. They'll struggle with managing their emotions if they use substances to regulate their feelings and must learn new coping skills to navigate their way through adolescence. They cannot shortcut their way through some of these struggles. Here are some additional points to remember:

- **Set clear boundaries.** Allow your child to go through their trials and tribulations. By allowing your child to manage their challenges, they will grow and learn. An important developmental task for youth is learning and mastering problem-solving. There's a difference between trying to take over the wheel versus offering a roadmap.

- **Promote open discussions and dialogue.** Understand what role your child wants you to play in their recovery. If they're struggling with their recovery and share that with you, don't overreact. Ask how you can help. At various times, a person can struggle with recovery. This is normal. That indicates an effort is being made toward abstaining and their sobriety means something to them. That is positive.

- **Ask open-ended questions, not yes or no ones.** Teenagers aren't passionate about sharing information with their parents. There's a difference between asking, "Did you have a good day?" and "Tell me about your day." The first answer will be yes, no, or I don't know. These types of exchanges don't lead to further discussion. The second at least allows some elaboration. You can open the door; your child must decide to walk through it.

- **Work on reestablishing trust.** In most cases, before the youth's commitment to abstaining, trust was broken. They used lies, avoidance, and deception to protect their use. It's not only okay but healthy for a parent to ask about their teen's journey in sobriety. Parents will need confirmation from their child that they're working on their recovery. Avoiding the topic with the child can not only indicate your disinterest but also re-create a communication pattern from when they were using (avoidance).

- **Develop your support systems.** Regardless of how committed your child may be to their recovery, their journey will be difficult for you as the parent. Support groups such as Al-Anon, community workshops, or religious institutions can also be helpful for parents. Knowing you're not alone can provide strength and hope.

- **Educate yourself as much as possible.** Aside from books and journals, some of your learning can come from support groups. Even attending an open meeting for addicts or alcoholics will give you some insight and show your support for your teen's recovery.

- **Provide structure and accountability.** Even if they're committed to abstaining, they're still teenagers. They need rules and direction from adults. Being in recovery does not give them a pass from being a teenager under the guidance of an adult (parent).

- **Work with the school to allow your child the best chance to succeed.** Because of their substance use, they could have fallen behind in their schooling. Schools will be accommodating in developing a plan to help your child catch up with their schoolwork. Not only will your child be playing catch up, but they will have challenges in concentration and focus, especially in early recovery.

- **Promote family time.** Have meals together. Go to activities as a family. This type of connection is essential to all youths, particularly those in recovery.

Keep in mind that there may be something else going on with your child aside from substance use. Regardless of whether you think your child's commitment to recovery is possible, they may be facing a mental health issue as well. At times, people may use substances to mask the symptoms they're feeling due to a mental health condition. This is a common occurrence at any age. The possibility of a co-occurring problem such as depression, anxiety, ADHD, etc., should be considered. It would be helpful to explore this possibility with treatment. Many individuals who develop substance use disorders are also diagnosed with mental disorders, and vice versa (20, 21). Although there are fewer studies on comorbidity among youth, research suggests that adolescents with substance use disorders also have high rates of co-occurring mental illness; over 60 percent of adolescents in community-based substance use disorder treatment programs also meet diagnostic criteria for another mental illness (22).

CHAPTER 12

Relapse

"Recovery is a process, not an event. We learn, we grow,
and we move forward. The decision to stop is just the first step.
The journey forward is the next step."

~Mark and Janet Myers

Unfortunately, due to the nature of substance use disorder, relapse is a complex but necessary discussion to cover. The reason we discuss this subject is not to assume those committed to stopping their use will inevitably relapse. Some individuals are successful in their first attempts at ceasing their use; others are not. We want to be careful not to assume a relapse will happen. We want to balance the reality of the situation and limit self-fulfilling prophecy.

If we view SUD as an illness (such as hypertension or asthma), the relapse rate is lower compared with other medical issues (23). The statistics vary regarding the success rate of recovery from SUD. The relapse rate ranges from 40 to 60 percent. Usually, in the first 90 days (about three months), the relapse rate is much higher in substance use recovery.

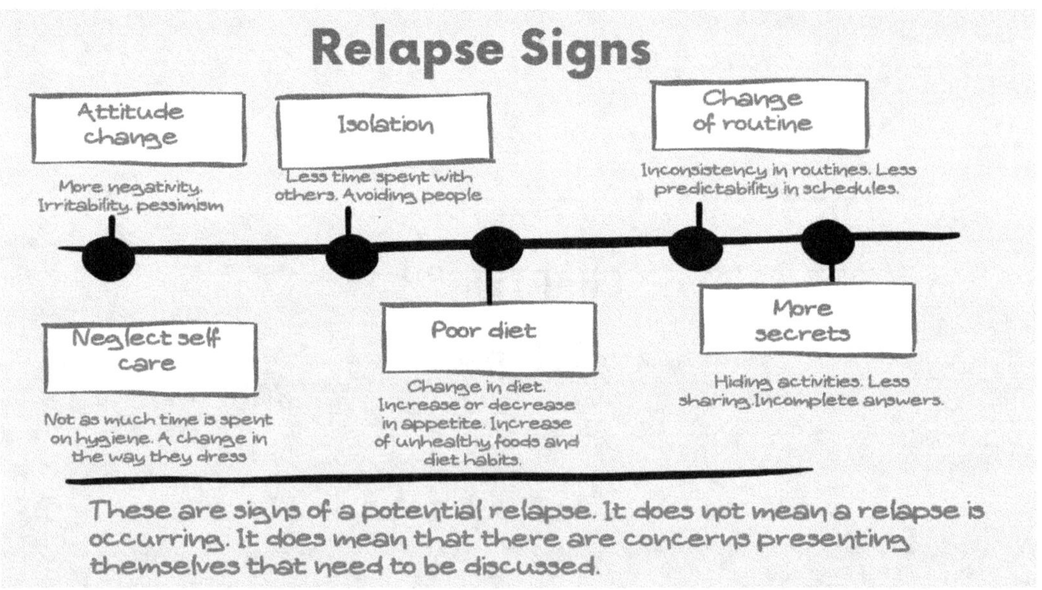

Types of Relapses

Professionals distinguish two types of relapses. The first is a lapse or slip. In this situation, the person has a short-lived, accidental deviation from the sobriety plan. They stumble and pick themself back up. The second type is called a traditional relapse and is defined as a decision to return to use. With either type, the user falls back into the same patterns and behaviors in which they engaged before they attempted abstinence. Whether it's a lapse/slip or traditional relapse is less important than how the family and user view the situation.

The decision to use is entirely different from a slip (see chart on Page 37). If it's a traditional relapse, the person with SUD is committed to continuing their use and not committed to a course of recovery. Families should look at this from a different lens than someone who is trying to stop and is not successful. Considering a user's response and actions, before and after the relapse, is more productive. It's a tricky road trying to define what we call a "violation of the recovering person's commitment to abstinence." On the one hand, if the user describes the incident as a slip, the family may feel the user is downplaying or minimizing the situation. If the family presents it as a relapse, the user may feel you're being over-reactive or not supportive.

A relapse can happen spontaneously. An event or situation presents itself, and the person uses. There was no prior buildup or any indications this would happen. In this case, the relapse can be attributed to poor planning, underestimating the challenge of maintaining sobriety, or something unforeseen.

There's an emotional and mental buildup that's experienced before the physical use happens. The emotional and mental relapse precedes the actual physical relapse.

Reactions to a Relapse

	Family	User
Thoughts	*Here we go again.* *Why are they doing this?* *What am I doing wrong?*	*I'm a failure.* *I'll never get their trust back.* *What's the point of trying to stay abstinent?*
Emotions	Anger, hurt, frustration, guilt, hopelessness	Guilt, shame, frustration, despair
Actions	Pulling away Yelling Blaming Talking about what happened	Defensive Blaming others Pulling away Decreased commitment to sobriety

It's important to understand that the user is responsible for their decision to use. The family's and user's responses to the relapse can either *fuel the relapse* episode or *help contain* it. The family members play a supportive role in the user's attempt to regroup from the relapse. Their response assists the user in rebounding from a relapse but can't cause it.

In most circumstances, a relapse should be viewed as a setback. For however long the loved one was abstinent, they have that successful time as a reference point on which to draw. Families and users can learn from their experience and hopefully minimize or prevent another relapse from happening. We should not view relapse as a failure.

The family will have to decide how they address the relapse. As we've discussed, each family is unique with experiences that shape their responses. For some, the healthy response will be distancing themselves from the user. Others find it productive to continue to be actively involved in their loved one's recovery. The responses will vary from one family to another.

Recovery is a process, not an event. We learn, we grow, and we move forward. The decision to stop is just the first step. The journey forward is the next step. If a relapse does happen:

- The family should talk openly about it. Don't hide what has happened. The user should share their feelings about the relapse. Since deception, secrecy, and avoidance are common in substance use, the topic of relapse should not be avoided.

- These questions are helpful to address:

    o What went wrong?

    o What changes need to take place and should be discussed?

    o What can the family do to support the user?

- The user needs to understand the impact the relapse has on the family. They should be patient and understand the family's disappointment and fears about the relapse.

- Determine if the treatment plan must introduce another level of care, additional tools, or examine medication. The level of care needed should be explored depending on the nature of the relapse (severity of relapse, substance of choice, length of relapse). This isn't to say there must be a step-up in services, but at least a discussion about that possibility is needed.

- For family members, focus on your self-care. You can be supportive, but not at your own expense. Taking care of yourself is a priority. A relapse, as well as past events associated with substance use, has a substantial emotional impact on family. You can't help the loved one or other family members while neglecting yourself.

- Identify and discuss potential risks and challenges in maintaining sobriety. Plan and predict situations that may be difficult. Both the user and the family should share these thoughts. Family members should be able to express their feelings about triggers they see or are concerned about.

- The family should seek professional help if they already haven't. What stops some family members from seeking out services for themselves is the belief the loved one's substance use is not their problem. Even though the family members aren't the ones causing the stress, they certainly feel the impact of the use. Professional help can also help the family decide their most productive course of action.

The road to recovery does not always go in a linear direction. It will take time, patience, and, most importantly, communication. The decision to move forward with or without the user will be difficult. Since we don't have a crystal ball, the future is unknown. A leap of faith in either direction, staying in the relationship, or leaving (if that's an option) are the choices family members will be facing.

Mount Recovery

Slips, unhealthy decisions, setbacks. Abstinence is not always a clear path. The climb can be difficult. The cost of not making the climb will be greater. Learn from your mistakes.

Some people can reach Mount Recovery involving no slips. Although it is the preferred route, it is often difficult for people to follow.

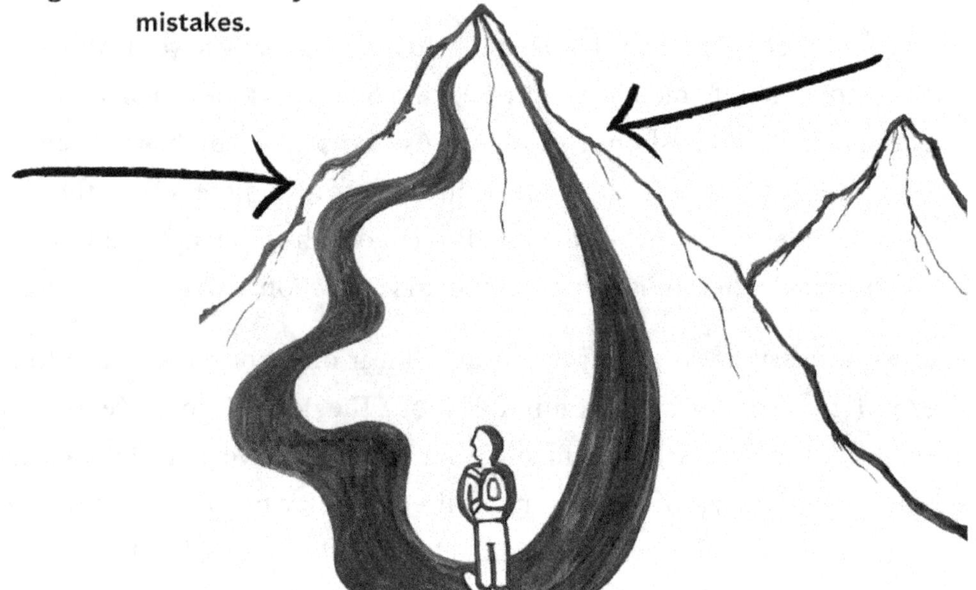

. . . . . .

CHAPTER 13

Exploring Treatment Options
for the User and Family

. . . . . .

"The opposite of addiction is not sobriety, but human connection."

~Author Unknown

Family members need to be involved in the process of seeking help for their treatment. The user's partner needs to be knowledgeable about available resources to assist in making informed treatment decisions. A good starting point is a thorough evaluation by an objective mental health professional who is willing to guide the family through the continuum of options available for treatment and how to access these resources. Family input into this process is vital.

Our conversation now leads us to exploring the role of professional help in the recovery journey. Getting involved in professional mental health counseling is strongly encouraged. Counseling benefits all parties in family recovery. The recovering user needs additional support to maximize their recovery. Having an objective and knowledgeable third party is necessary. Therapy provides needed support and guidance. Family counseling helps facilitate communications that have been hampered by substance use. In most cases, both are helpful.

Treatment and Therapeutic Resources

Depending on the severity, duration, and frequency of the substance use, the user may need more intensive services. There are different levels of care available for those seeking professional help. We'll discuss these in detail in the next chapter. For now, we'll include options led by professional mental health providers and those led by volunteers.

Self-help groups: These groups are peer-led and don't have any professionals involved. They are facilitated by volunteers with substance use issues who have used the group for their own recovery. A self-help group is recommended as part of a recovery plan to assist the user and in many cases family members to develop and support non-using behaviors. The most abundant type of self-help group available is the twelve-step. There are multiple types of 12-step groups available, specific to the substance a person uses.

. For teens, we recommend looking for a group geared toward young people. Self-help groups are most useful for teens who identify they have a problem and actively engaged in recovery. This type of group relies on peers helping peers and can be counterproductive for people who refuse to actively participate. In most situations, additional support (see below) should be offered.

Outpatient counseling: This usually includes individual, family, and/or couple counseling. The treatment and frequency of sessions vary depending on the needs of the family. Often, it's a combination of these three. Master's degree or a licensed professional render these services. Make sure the therapist is a certified substance abuse counselor or at least has some expertise in this area.

Outpatient group counseling: Some communities offer outpatient group counseling. These services are offered at a clinic or private practice setting and meet once or twice a week. A professional counselor leads these group meetings. Group counseling occurs in other settings, such as residential, inpatient, or intensive outpatient settings. These groups are part of that treatment setting and not available unless the recovering person is part of that setting. We will explain further in the next section.

Intensive outpatient counseling: This usually consists of 12-15 hours a week. Most of the services in this setting are offered through group meetings. There will also be some individual counseling and family, but group counseling is usually the main approach. Educational lectures are also included, both for the family and the individual. If this is a family's choice, we strongly encourage active involvement in this model. We cannot stress enough the importance of family participation in the treatment process, especially parents.

Partial hospitalization or day program: This type of therapy is a full day of programming. Group, individual, education, and other types of treatment are conducted in these settings. Professionals staff this type of program. It takes place in a hospital or treatment center. The participants stay in the setting most of the day and return to their homes at the end of the day. As with Intensive outpatient (IOP), and inpatient hospitalization, active family participation and involvement improves treatment outcomes.

Inpatient hospitalization: Programming is similar to a day program described above. The difference is the recovering individual stays overnight. The length of time someone would remain in this type of treatment will depend on the facility and the insurance (if that's how the hospital stay is funded). Most insurance looks at this type of treatment as a short-term approach. They want to stabilize the person and move them to something less restrictive (day program or something else). The length of stay can be three days (at the short end) to 10 days (at the long end). Active engagement of family members throughout the treatment process sets the stage for a healthy transition to home and other treatment resources to support sobriety in the community.

Medication management (medication-assisted therapy): Medication can help drug and alcohol patients detox from a drug or manage their cravings. As we mentioned before, if there were a coexisting disorder, doctors would recommend medication to assist in stabilizing their mental health symptoms as well. It's essential to have a psychiatrist (not a primary care physician) prescribe medication, especially for young people. Introducing medication for all clients, but especially the developing brains of younger people, should be mindfully explored. The complexities of addressing and medicating both mental health and substance abuse issues dictate that it needs to be carried out with someone who has significant knowledge and expertise. We strongly encourage that this type of treatment be supplemented by other types of modalities, at least in the beginning portion of treatment. Medication without other types of services can have limited results, especially in the early part of recovery. Once there is continued sobriety, tapering back or eliminating other treatment modalities can be done once the youth is stabilized.

Residential: This is a longer-term setting. The length of stay varies but has the longest stay of any other type of treatment. There are numerous methods of therapy services offered in this setting. It has similar components to the inpatient and partial hospital settings but occurs for a longer period. This setting provides the highest level of structure and the most intensive services. It's important that families understand this is not a starting point for treatment unless there is a life-threatening SUD. It can be counterproductive to start with this level of care unless it is absolutely necessary because of exposure to other users in need of intensive services.

Support and Therapy for Teens

Getting help for teens has its own special considerations. If your child doesn't voluntarily want to go into therapy/treatment, parents do have the legal right to mandate it. Laws vary by state, and we recommend looking into your state's approach to involuntary admission for youth.

Parents will have to weigh out the costs and benefits of doing this. If the youth is involved with the courts, they can enforce them to go into therapy or treatment. Parents can use an intensive outpatient or residential program without court involvement. Insurance, in most situations, can cover at least a portion of the costs. Most facilities will give you a cost breakdown and your expected fees.

Mandating treatment is a big decision that parents should mindfully approach. Before pursuing this route, we recommend talking to a professional who is a neutral third party. They can help guide you in deciding the best course of action to take. Professionals can help you evaluate the decision, as well as the facility. We suggest a facility with a family therapy component and a good after-care approach. The treatment facility options can vary depending on your geographical location and your resources. Knowing which facility to use will not only depend on where the user lives, but also the financial flexibility that is available. Treatment facilities are expensive and depending on the type of treatment needed may cost substantial amounts of money. It is very important that families carefully evaluate their options.

Creating a Network of Support for the Recovering Individual and the Family

Working together creates greater productivity and ensures our safety as a species. We learned this from early hunter/gatherer societies that being in community with others protects us from predators and helps us meet our collective needs. We continue to live, work and play in groups today. Forming connections allows us to work through the difficulties of life.

The benefits of feeling connected range from helping us deal with medical conditions such as cancer, obesity, blood pressure and pain management to lowering the risk of dementia and improving our immune system, just to name a few. From a mental health perspective, friendships in our teen years are important in the prevention of mental health issues as we become adults, and overall emotional well-being.

Feeling socially connected and *being* socially connected are different. You could belong to an extensive network of friends and relationships, but if you don't have a shared sense of purpose, meaning, trust, and support, just physically being in a group doesn't guarantee you'll feel a part of it. The number of social connections is not as important as how you feel about the group and how helpful that group is for you, i.e., the *quality* of the relationships.

You don't have to get all your emotional needs met by one group or person. You may have great connections in groups from your past such as high school friends, a previous job, or from a past season in your life (e.g., divorce group). How frequently you participate in these groups is less important than what you get out of them. People develop their support systems based on a variety of factors and our history often determines the connections between people.

Substance abuse has devastating effects on families for the user and loved ones, including the loss of support networks. Isolation is a common problem in recovering families. Users may need to discontinue their association with people who, in the past, played significant roles in their lives. As a result, family members may also lose valuable connections for a variety of reasons, based on the following:

- Loved ones fear what the extended family and friends will think of them or the user. They worry they will be judged.

- The family will want to protect the user. They believe the user's reputation or status won't be harmed if they keep this information hidden from extended family and friends.

- The family's support systems feel exhausted from hearing about the user. They're burnt out or frustrated from the highs and lows they've heard about and gone through coming from the user's significant other.

- The substance users themselves will try to isolate the family from outside support. They benefit from this isolation as that can weaken the resolve of their family to address the substance abuse issue. This allows the user to continue using with less conflict regarding their use. They keep information exclusively within the family, preventing outside influences from threatening the family's secrets.

Identifying a Support System Worksheet

Identifying a support system can be challenging. Families tend to be concerned about letting others into their world. Having a network of support provides family members valuable outlets for managing the stress of recovery from substance use disorder. Each family member needs their own support and resources for themselves as well as the entire family.

Use this template to create your own version of your family's support network.

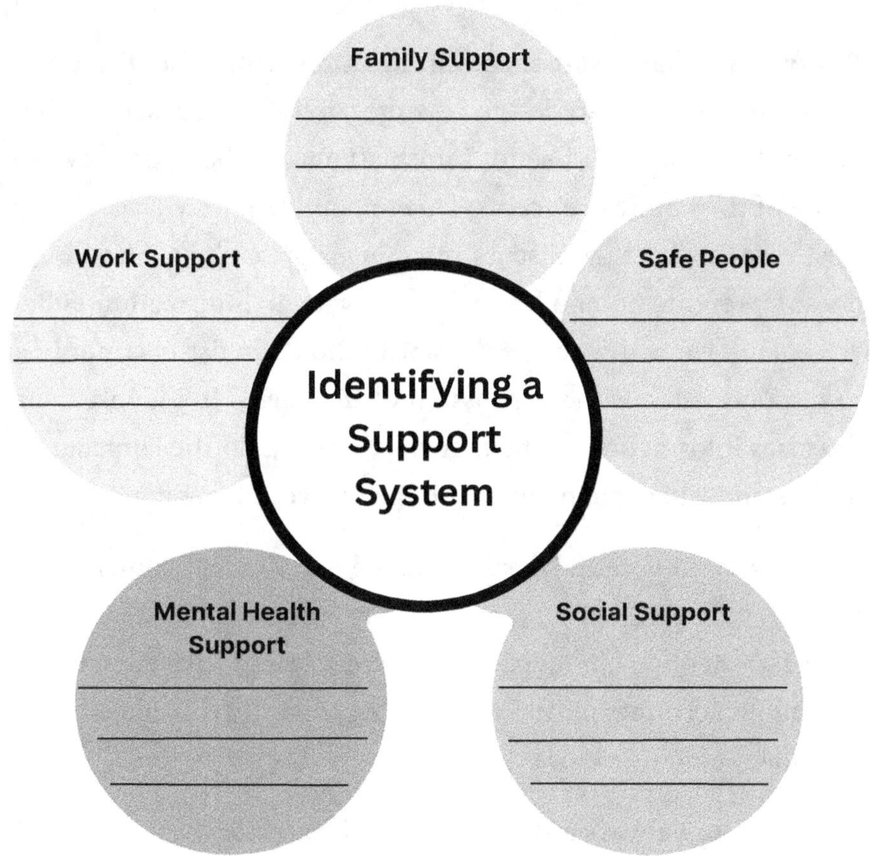

Notes for the Journey Home

Treatment and accountability are the important tools that help users free themselves from substance use disorder. Helping them on the journey requires family members to patiently set and enforce limits that support sober living within the home.

- **Enforce therapy.** Families can use consequences, such as asking someone to move out if they refuse to go to therapy. If the user refuses to participate in counseling, a parent or other family member may have little leverage.

- **Ensure you have some communication with the therapist.** If counseling sessions are left to the integrity of the substance-abusing person to disclose all helpful information, the therapist may not be aware of the family's concerns. Due to confidentiality laws, therapists can't reveal what they discuss in counseling sessions. However, that doesn't prevent the family from sharing their information either by voicemail or email with the therapist. The therapist may not be able to respond without the permission of the client. If a family member discloses information to the therapist, it will help the clinician better understand what's happening with the recovering person.

- **Urinalysis and breathalyzers** should be part of the treatment process. For the user invested in their recovery, they'll understand this is a necessary step in gaining back trust. For a less motivated person, this will allow accountability. In the next chapter, we've included some information on urinalysis.

- **Recovery isn't always a straight upward trajectory.** Sometimes, there are slips. If a slip does happen, remain positive. For a user struggling with recovery, it would be deflating if they felt their family had given up on them.

- **Distinguish between *can't* and *won't* in stopping their use.** The way a family confronts the user will depend on how they view the user's efforts in maintaining abstinence. If the user tries to stop using and fail, your approach is different than if they refused to stop using.

· · · · · ·

CHAPTER 14

Developing a Support System

· · · · · ·

**"Families need the support and validation of others
to gain a healthy perspective."**
~Mark and Janet Myers

For family members experiencing the impact of a loved one's SUD, developing a support system is crucial. Families need the encouragement and validation of others to gain a healthy perspective. The user should have a variety of supports that will allow them to learn and develop new skills and behaviors. Families should also be educated regarding treatment options for their loved one.

There are two types of groups or support systems. Those are peer-led **self-help groups** and professionally led **support groups**.

Both types of groups present similar structures:

For peer-led **self-help groups**, finding them can be relatively easy. A google search turns up several local meetings in the area. The makeup of groups will depend on the demographic differences in your area. Most groups will have a description that will inform you to some extent of the type of group you'll be attending. Also, remember that although all the self-help groups follow a specific structure, group leader styles can differ. Attending one meeting only won't give you enough information on which to base a decision whether or not it will be a good fit for you. We encourage attending a few sessions with different times, locations, and group leaders. Keep in mind that not everyone will find self-help groups productive. It's important to give them a try, or at least consider one.

Twelve-step self-help groups are the most available type. Twelve-step refers to any self-help group that uses a 12-step model in its treatment philosophy. These groups all have their roots in Alcoholics Anonymous (A.A.). Since A.A.'s incorporation, the 12-step model has been used to address various platforms, including, but not limited to, Gamblers Anonymous, Narcotics Anonymous, Cocaine Anonymous, and Families Anonymous. The list is long and goes beyond the few we mentioned. The model centers around the participant starting at the first step and working to the twelfth step with the support of their group. After completing the twelfth step, they begin to work through the steps again from the beginning. Each step has its challenges and tasks for the person to address.

Support groups are more challenging to locate. A general search on the internet will provide information for professionally led support groups in your area. Social media provides some directions for finding a support group close to you. Facebook, Reddit, and Meetup (meetup.com) also offer resources. When you're conducting your searches, do some vetting of their programs and curriculum. Look for the therapist's credentials, group goals, and number of participants. Professionals, friends, and self-help group members are other resources to explore. Religious institutions can also be helpful in your search. It's important to understand the difference between a support group and a self-help group. Although they both can be helpful, they serve different purposes. We include this chart to distinguish between the two.

Group Descriptions

	Self-Help Group	**Support Group**
Group leaders	Peer-led. Group leader(s) have gone through the experience of SUD.	May have more than one professional group leader. Educational level is usually the minimum of a bachelor's degree in a mental health field. Most typically, a master's degree.
Length of group	Typically lasts 1½ - 2 hours. The same self-help group will meet once a week. Participants attend more than once a week. Groups are open-ended, meaning they have no official start date or end date.	Typically runs for 90 minutes (about 1½ - 2 hours). Usually meets once a week. Time-limited (8 to 16 weeks). Once a group concludes, leaders can start another group. Has a set number of group sessions. Participants need to commit to attending for the length of the group. In some circumstances, participants can repeat the same group.
Cost of group	Free. Some groups will pass around a donation plate to cover the costs of coffee. Contributions are voluntary.	Costs to attend. Fees can vary depending on who is offering the group. Insurance may cover a portion of the costs.
Availability of group	Some are available 24 hours a day, e.g., Alcoholics Anonymous. Other self-help groups are less available. Offered online or in person.	Tend to run in cycles. Length of group, typically 8-16 weeks. The same group is offered again at a later point. In most cases, participants are offered choices regarding times and locations.
Number of participants	Unlimited. If it's an online group, up to 40 or more people may attend.	Group size is usually 6-10 participants. The people running these groups will limit the size to maximize the benefits of the group's goals.
Location of group	Online or in person. Found throughout the community. Some churches or organizations donate space for groups to conduct their meetings.	Hospitals, community centers, or private practice settings.
Focus of the group	Most have a general objective determining the structure or what to expect from the meeting. E.g., some Alcoholics Anonymous meetings offer a First Step Group, specifically focusing on the first step in the 12-step model. Other groups are not 12-step based.	Direct and targeted. Group leaders have stated goals and objectives. Specific skills, strategies, and techniques will address their areas of concern. Traditionally more structured than self-help groups.

Home Pages

We have included the home pages where you can find meetings as well as a general description of various groups.

Adult Children of Alcoholics: https://adultchildren.org/ This is a 12-step program for people who grew up in a substance-abusing (or other types of abuse) family.

Al-Anon: https://al-anon.org/ Al-Anon members are worried about someone with a drinking problem and want to help them. Learn from the experiences of others, find effective ways to cope, and join meetings near you.

Codependent Anonymous: https://coda.org/ is a 12-step support group for people who are trying to regain healthy relationships with themselves and others after experiencing the challenges of another's addiction.

Celebrate Recovery: https://www.celebraterecovery.com/ is a faith-based 12-step recovery program for anyone struggling with any type of addictive behavior or mental health issues.

Families Anonymous (FA): https://familiesanonymous.org/ FA is a 12-step fellowship for the family and friends of those with drug, alcohol, or related behavioral issues.

Families of Addicts (FOA): https://foafamilies.org/ Families, individuals in recovery, and those seeking recovery meet together. This unique approach fosters a better understanding of how addiction affects every family member. FOA connects people to treatment and provides access to resources that have been thoroughly vetted.

Learn to Cope: https://learn2cope.org/ Learn to Cope is a peer-led support group for family members and friends who have loved ones affected by substance abuse.

Nar-Anon: https://www.nar-anon.org/. The Nar-Anon Family Group is primarily for those who know or have known a feeling of desperation concerning the addiction problem of someone very near to you.

Nara Teen: https://www.nar-anon.org/ Narateen is part of the Nar-Anon program for teens affected by someone else›s addiction. You can find more information about this group through the Nar-Anon site.

Parents of Addicted Loved Ones (PALS):https://palgroup.org/ PAL Group is a nonprofit that offers education and support to parents of adults with substance use disorder. Learn how to help your child, improve your health and well-being, and find hope through weekly meetings and online resources.

Recovering Couples Anonymous: https://recovering-couples.org/ Recovering Couples Anonymous provides support for couples affected by substance abuse to help restore healthy communication and greater intimacy. Although they're not affiliated with Alcoholics Anonymous, their system is based on that of A.A.

Smart Recovery: https://smartrecovery.org/ Recovery Family & Friends is a science-based program for family members of people living with addiction. SMART Recovery Family & Friends has several meetings in many cities and uses non-confrontational methods to help loved ones cope with a friend or family member's addiction.

Teen Corner: https://al-anon.org/newcomers/teen-corner-alateen/ This site is accessed through Al-Anon. It is a place for teens affected by someone else's alcoholism.

Deciding on a Course of Action

Families must make tough decisions about the level of care. We encourage individuals and their families to weigh out their options. Offering someone more services that they need can be just as counterproductive as letting the issue go untreated. Unless there are safety risks, such as risk of overdose, we prefer to start at the least restrictive end of the service continuum. Prior treatment experiences, level of use, history of use, substance they're using, availability of resources, and other factors need to be considered in determining what level of care best addresses their use.

We recommend talking to a professional when deciding to pursue treatment. If you start from the least restrictive setting, we suggest setting up criteria to determine if this would be the best place to start for your family member. If the client is going to start with outpatient counseling, get an agreement ahead of time with their therapist to evaluate the effectiveness of this level of care at a specified point during treatment. For instance, if they relapse (use again), they would agree to go to a more restrictive setting (intensive outpatient). The contract should be tailored to the specific needs and circumstances of the client and family. Evaluating the level of care with family members requires transparency on the part of the recovering person.

The client's level of motivation needs to be considered when choosing the level of care. We discussed how external factors will typically drive a client to counseling. If there is a relapse, it's important to determine if it was a decision to use substances again, or if they were trying to stay abstinent and they slipped.

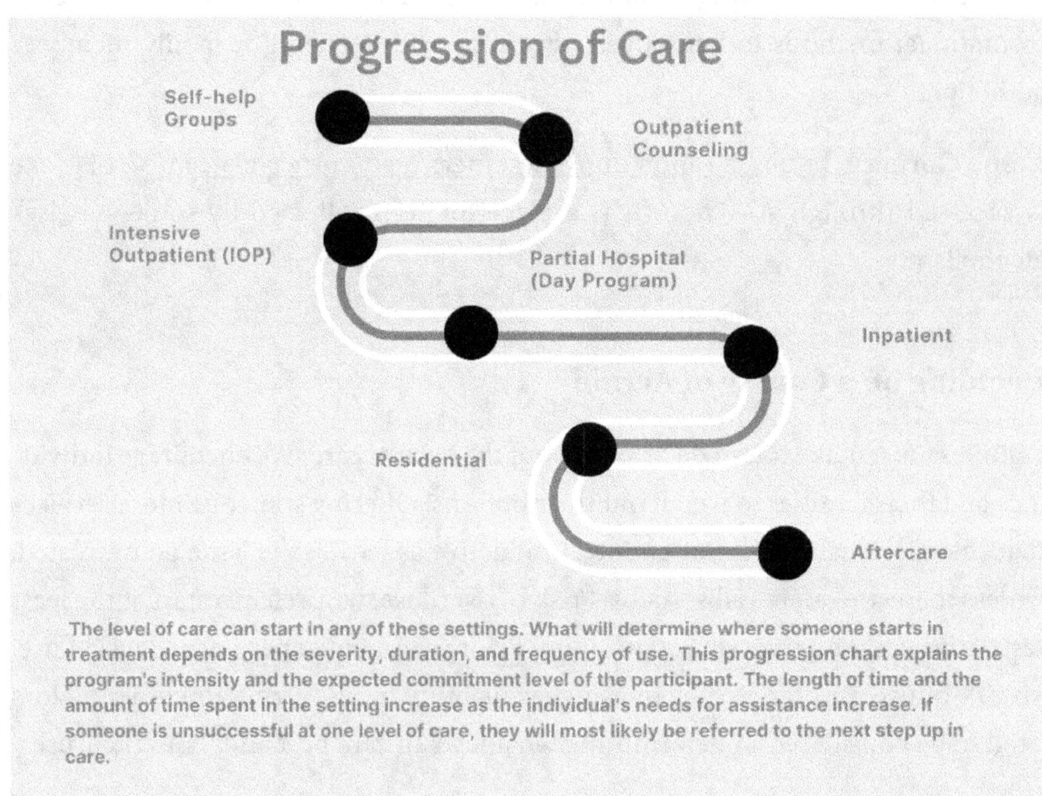

The level of care can start in any of these settings. What will determine where someone starts in treatment depends on the severity, duration, and frequency of use. This progression chart explains the program's intensity and the expected commitment level of the participant. The length of time and the amount of time spent in the setting increase as the individual's needs for assistance increase. If someone is unsuccessful at one level of care, they will most likely be referred to the next step up in care.

LEVEL OF CARE

Too Intensive	Not Intensive Enough
Too much too soon If the person relapses, there might not be other treatment options available.	**Risk Factor** Individuals are at a safety risk. The impact of their relapse would be dangerous.
Using it all up Individuals tap into resources. This includes financial, child care, and other components.	**Relapse potential** The individual needs are greater than what is being offered. The individual is at a greater risk for relapse
Dropping out Individual loses interest. It is difficult for them to continue to put in the time and energy. They do not believe it is necessary.	**Unmet concerns** An individual has a mental health issue that goes undiagnosed. It becomes difficult for them to manage the substance abuse and the mental health issue.
Unsuccessful in maintaining abstinence by themselves. Individual feels they were not able to try this on their own. They lose their belief they could do it their own way. Loss of their own input into the decision.	**External factors** Their use impacts their employment, legal status, or family life. The consequences of use are substantial.

Drug Screening

Periodic drug screening is a helpful tool for substance users and their families. Drug screening also includes breathalyzers. You can find a breakdown of the different types of drug screenings available on Page 149 in this chapter. We've also included the length of time each substance stays in the body. There are several benefits to testing in therapy:

- It offers accountability. The substance user is taking responsibility for the behavior (substance use) that created stress for the family.

- The user, by complying with drug screens, demonstrates their willingness to build back trust in the family.

- It reassures families the user is committed to staying abstinent. If they're suspicious that their loved one has been using substances, drug screens will let the family know they haven't been using.

- If there are relapses (or use), positive drug screens mean that information can be discussed earlier rather than later. A positive result allows a dialogue between the user and the family member to discuss the meaning and circumstances behind the positive screen. Since shame, guilt, and avoidance are common in substance use disorders, this information can be helpful to process the use and discuss the next course of action.

- The substance user won't have to prove their innocence. If the family member suspects there's been a relapse and there wasn't one, the user will have a difficult time proving they didn't use. A drug screen makes it clear whether they did or didn't and avoids arguments trying to prove one way or the other.

- There are times where the substance user themself will find the screens helpful. This accountability can help keep them pointed in a direction of abstinence.

Family members need to focus on grounding themselves as well. We cannot help your loved one through their struggles with SUD unless you emotionally tend to your needs. There are tremendous obstacles and choices you'll have to navigate. You don't have to face them alone.

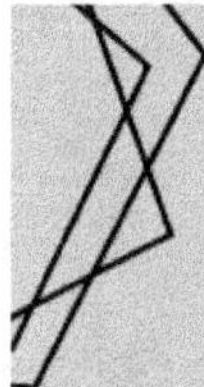

DIFFERENT TYPES OF DRUG SCREENING

URINE

- The most reliable and frequently used method
- Can be invasive as most require observation during sample collection to prevent tampering
- Administered by a professional
- Provides accurate results of recent drug use

ORAL

- Easy to administer
- Less invasive than urine screening
- Difficult to alter the sample, ensuring accuracy
- May not detect long-term substance use due to shorter detection time
- Results are fast and accessible to give on-site

HAIR

- Cannot detect recent use
- Can detect the longest window of substance use, typically up to 90 days
- More expensive and results may take longer
- Results may be less reliable than other tests
- Close observation during collection minimizes the risk of sample manipulation.

Drug	Urine	Hair	Oral
Alcohol	7-12 hours	90 days	24-78 hours
Amphetamines	2-3 days	90 days	5-48 hours
Benzodiazepines (Short-acting)	2 days	90 days	5-48 hours
Benzodiazepines (Intermediate- acting)	5 days	90 days	5-48 hours
Benzodiazepines (Long-acting)	10-30 days	90 days	5-48 hours
Cannabinoids	3-30 days	90 days	7-21 hours
Cocaine metabolites	1-3 days	90 days	5-48 days
Opioids	2-3 days	90 days	7-21 hours
Phenylcyclidine (Angel Dust)	8 days	90 days	5-48 hours

Notes for the Journey Home

For family members experiencing the impact of a loved one's SUD, developing a support system is crucial. Families need the support and validation of others to gain a healthy perspective. There are similarities between self-help and support groups in the benefits gained from attending. These benefits include:

- Validation. For both the user and the family impacted by SUD, knowing others have experienced what you're going through enormously impacts your emotional well-being.

- These settings will allow you to share your feelings in a safe place. Keeping these thoughts to yourself causes your experience to continue weighing on you and your family.

- Participants can gain knowledge and skills from other (or group leaders') experiences.

- Family members will better understand what they're dealing with. Knowing this will help them better prepare for events they may face.

- Support groups create more self-confidence in your decision-making. Knowing a group is behind a decision or belief you have is empowering. Participants don't have to feel alone. The support of your group backs you.

- The family learns to separate themselves from feeling responsible for the substance abuse.

- Often, group members, whether the user or the family, can develop a solid social network. Regardless of which group you attend, the potential to expand your resources is excellent. The connectivity members experience in these groups can create lasting friendships and support.

Seeking outside help is tremendously helpful for those in recovery and their family members. Children can also benefit from these groups. Which group you attend is up to either the user or the family member, depending on the group. Getting to the group could mean overcoming your self-imposed mental barriers. Sharing your experiences in a safe and supportive environment will help you navigate the challenges you face.

· · · · · · ·

CHAPTER 15

Home

· · · · · · ·

"Recovery is about progression, not perfection."

– Unknown

Have you ever traveled far from home and couldn't wait to return to a familiar, comforting, peaceful place? Some of us may have yet to experience home that way. Recovery offers the possibility of a new home of safety and peace. How we accomplish this is our journey in recovery. Each path looks different because the people are different.

We've taken you through the stages of family recovery, introduced you to the challenges, and shared tools to help you in your travels. Healing from substance use takes time and commitment. Embracing the whole of it is vital to finding a home that meets your family's needs. Take time to review and reflect on the process of recovery.

1. **Recognize the path.** Delving into family recovery leads us in a direction of discovery that changes the trajectory of our lives and relationships. Recovery requires honesty and transparency. Each family member must examine their role. You will each accomplish this goal at your own pace.

2. **Embrace change.** It is natural to fear change and experience resistance, saying, "I'm not the one who did this to us. Why do I need to change?" Ultimately, all people change over time, and it's your choice to be willing or unwilling to participate. Small actions lead to significant changes over time. Allow yourself to look at your life with honesty, gentleness, and kindness, then choose to make small changes.

3. **Give yourself time to adapt.** Remember, rewiring ourselves takes time, patience, and rehearsal. The more frequently you rehearse new behaviors and thoughts, the more you cement your new path, including new ways of thinking and interacting with family.

4. **Allow flexibility.** Home may not look the same when you get there; the people and what you want from one another will evolve. Growing together is possible.

Recovery, as we have previously mentioned, isn't always a direct upward trajectory—in fact, many times it fluctuates in a non-linear path. Families will experience their ups and downs, especially in early recovery. They need to establish new roles. They need to re-earn trust. Restoring communication and rebuilding confidence in one another occurs with practice. Triggers need to be managed, both from the user and the family. Indeed, the road to recovery will not be easy. However, it's vital to remember that this is a path families must take. The other option is allowing the use to go unchecked, leaving families caught up in the black hole of addiction.

Preparing for the challenges of recovery doesn't mean a lifetime of looking over your shoulder. At some point, family members need to let go of trying to determine if or when a relapse or setback will occur. If someone is always worried about tomorrow or what's next, they'll lose out on living and enjoying today.

Your family may not remain intact in your journey of recovery. Unfortunately, that is the reality of substance abuse. However, you won't know your situation unless you commit to the journey. A lot of families grow more robust—stronger after managing the challenges of recovery.

Home is a metaphor. It's a place where you feel safe and connected. It's an internal destination, not an external one. Finding your way in recovery will land you somewhere different from where you started. Not necessarily better or worse, but different. The journey begins by taking that first step in acknowledging the problem. This action depends on a choice each individual makes, whether it's the user or family member, and it doesn't require others to commit to the same path as you. It would be nice if they did, but that doesn't have to be a factor in your recovery. The journey begins when you are no longer looking behind but accepting today, looking forward to tomorrow, and not focusing on what is next.

As we journey through the challenges of substance use disorder, it leaves us in a completely new place. Whether you end up living in the same house or a different one—with or without the people you started with—home can be a place of joy and safety. Although we long at times for the familiar, we hope for change that often leads us to a new home, a place we've never been.

Sobriety requires shifts in thinking and behavior for everyone. Some of the journey will be uncomfortable. Families recover at different speeds. As a result, it's possible that family members end up in other places. In our practice, we work with families and substance users. Some families recover together with growing pains. Some families recover separately as individuals within the family and go their own way. We hope your home experiences happier people, safer behaviors, improved relationships, and healthier boundaries as a result of doing the hard work of journeying through recovery.

Stories of the Journey Home

"The journey of a thousand miles begins with one step."

~Lao Tzu

Here are some final thoughts. We have covered in this book, as well as our previous book *Falling Trees, Color Blind Scientists & Addiction*, the impact substance use disorders can have on individuals and families. The journey can be difficult but is not impossible. The substance abuse recovery journey affects many people. Numerous celebrities have had their experiences with substances and are sober today. Readers can google Demi Lovato, Jamie Lee Curtis, Elton John, and Daniel Radcliff, to name just a few.

Robert John Downey Jr. (born April 4, 1965) is an American actor. Most people who prefer the superhero genre recognize him from his role as Marvel's *Iron Man*. Some of his earlier works included *Weird Science* (1985), *Less Than Zero* (1987), and *Charlie Chaplin* (1992). However, even though he enjoyed some success early in his career, he struggled with a substance use problem. His problems started at age eight, according to Downey. He says that his father, who reportedly had a substance abuse problem, gave him marijuana at age 6.

When he was making the movie *Less Than Zero*, he was involved in heavy substance use. "It was just a wild era," said Downey Jr. "That whole world, it gets tied into creativity. We were all altering our consciousness with substances. I was just kinda playing a game of just wanting to self-soothe or just stay loaded rather than deal with the fact that things had gone off the tracks a little bit." ([https://people.](https://people.com/movies/robert-downey-jr-recalls-drug-addiction-sr-documentary/) [com/movies/robert-downey-jr-recalls-drug-addiction-sr-documentary/](https://people.com/movies/robert-downey-jr-recalls-drug-addiction-sr-documentary/)). Some of it he attributes to the culture he grew up in.

His first arrest was in 1996 for possession of heroin, cocaine, and an unloaded .357 Magnum. He was given three years of probation and required to undergo mandatory drug testing. Also, that year, his neighbors found him passed out in their 11-year-old's bed. No charges were pressed. A year later he skipped a drug test and spent four months in jail. He skipped another drug test and was sentenced to three years of prison. He wound up serving 15 months of that sentence.

Four months later, after his release, he was arrested again. This time for cocaine and valium possession and being under the influence of drugs. In April of 2000, he was arrested again for wandering in an alleyway.

Aside from all these arrests, his reputation in Hollywood caused movie companies not to want to hire him. After committing to sobriety during the 2003 filming of *The Singing Detective*, he returned to the screen. The director, Mel Gibson, had to pay his insurance bond for the film, as no insurance company would insure him. This led to other roles and eventually to *Iron Man* (2007). Today, he is one of the highest-paid actors in Hollywood. He has been drug-free since 2003.

Downey said the turning point was when his wife gave him an ultimatum to quit drugs. "You think [overcoming addiction is] supposed to get more and more dramatic, it's not a movie. It's real life. For me, I just happened to be in a situation the very last time and I said, 'You know what? I don't think I can continue doing this.' And I reached out for help and I ran with it, you know? … It's not that difficult to overcome these seemingly ghastly problems. … What's hard is to decide."

In this section, we will share some stories of people we have worked with over the years. The names and situations have been altered enough to protect their confidentiality. However, readers will still have a good picture of their struggles and triumphs.

Jim, when I first met with him, was a 21-year-old who came to therapy for anxiety. Initially, he presented concerns about his anxiety. He was experiencing significant stress, particularly in social situations. At the time, he was living with his parents. He was going part-time to a community college. He reported some episodes of drinking but denied it was a problem.

We were initially focusing on his anxiety. We worked with different treatment approaches, which seemed to help. However, as treatment progressed, there were some clear concerns about his drinking. He reported several incidents of over-drinking. Reluctant to address this directly in counseling, Jim was evasive and resistant to in-depth discussions about his drinking. In therapy, it is important to work where the client wants to start and work on what they are willing to address. Although therapists recognize there may be a problem, we are limited in how much we can get them to work through if they don't want to or can't focus on certain issues.

After a few months of seeing him, he informed me that his parents wanted to have a family session. He stated his parents had concerns about his drinking. Due to confidentiality rules in therapy, therapists are restricted in what they can share with the parents. However, we can listen to what others have to say. The parents presented concerns about his drinking that occurred over several years. This was information that Jim did not share in our initial sessions.

Jim began to open up about his drinking. He shared even more concerns and incidents than his parents presented. Jim's drinking turned into a focus of counseling. He realized how his drinking created more problems for him and he was using it to self-medicate. After several attempts at moderating and trying to stop, Jim entered a treatment center. He completed the program.

At this writing, Jim has seven years of sobriety. He still has some anxiety but can manage it healthily. Recently, he married his high school sweetheart and is expecting a baby soon. Once Jim committed to focusing on his drinking, he was able to recognize how destructive it was and how it impacted the way he managed his anxiety. Involving his parents in the journey changed the trajectory of treatment and made it possible for him to look critically at his drinking and the impact it had on others.

Wendy is a middle-aged woman who has been married for over 20 years. She and her husband have four young adult children. She was seeking out treatment due to her discovery that her husband was actively using cocaine for over ten years. The family didn't recognize any of this until it came to Wendy's attention that he had tapped into the children's college accounts and their retirement account. Furthermore, she discovered that he had also paid for prostitutes when he was actively using.

Initially, the husband denied he was actively using. He was offering excuses and denials about his use and where the money went. All the children knew about the circumstances of what the father/husband had done. They had sought out family counseling to sort through the events and decide on a course of action moving forward.

The initial sessions focused around the family understanding the nature of substance abuse. At first there was a lot of self-blame and anger that they hadn't seen evidence of the problem before it reached the point it did. They were also confused at how their father/husband would seem so sincere in presenting his version of events, yet they saw something entirely different.

As therapy progressed, each family member sorted out the events that led up to treatment and deciding what type of relationship they were going to have with the husband/father. They were able to spend less time getting caught up with proving him wrong in what he was saying and realizing the limitations of their relationship while he was avoiding any responsibility or accountability for his actions.

The couple wound up divorcing. Three of the children have decided not to have a relationship with him. The fourth child is keeping him at an arm's distance. They have spent considerably less time trying to prove his lies. They have accepted that unless the kids see clear efforts on his part about accountability and responsibility for what he has done, they're not going to invest in the relationship. Wendy has stopped blaming herself and has gained more confidence in herself. She has also attended Al-Anon and found it helpful to hear and be supported by others. She doesn't feel alone.

On a personal level, we asked our sister or sister-in-law about contributing to our book. Initially, we weren't sure about putting her in the position to share her story. Karen didn't hesitate in our request. We appreciate the courage she has in her willingness to share her story, which has a prequel. Our parents and grandparents also struggled with substance use disorder.

Ray was the youngest born child of two Swedish immigrants. His father Oscar was a bricklayer and his mother Stina was a waitress, a hostess, and later an administrator for a home for the aged. They were hard working and raised their children in church. They were also both alcoholics who had frequent arguments that became physically abusive. Stina was a petite woman who was easily overpowered. The abuse eventually stopped when their younger son Ray began to fight back on his mother's behalf and had grown taller and stronger than his father.

They moved to Florida after they retired. Both Oscar and Stina continued to drink off and on throughout the years in an almost symbiotic way. Stina was unable to stay sober when Oscar wasn't there to monitor her behavior. On several occasions, she was found by family members injured and drunk after a drinking binge. When Oscar died, her sons moved her from Florida to Illinois to be closer to her. Unfortunately, Oscar had hidden that she was suffering from Alzheimer's. She kept drinking as long as she was independent, then slowly slipped away.

Ray's drinking started when he was 11 or 12 years old, with beer, and escalated throughout his life. He met his wife Ruth when she was 17 and he was 18. He entered the Navy not long after they met. They continued to date until they married in 1959. She went to nursing school and they started a family in 1964. They were largely social drinkers and this became more and more problematic over time. He had problems with managing frustration and anger, and though he was never physically aggressive with Ruth, he was harsh in his discipline of their four children. He tried many times to moderate and quit his drinking but returned to it. He had trouble getting through the day without drinking and had bottles of liquor hidden all over the house. Finally, in 1982, Ruth had enough and gave Ray an ultimatum. They both stopped drinking and though Ruth did not have an alcohol problem, she supported Ray by not drinking. He had some relapses, and each time they worked through it together. Ruth and Ray were married for 51 years before his death to cancer, and he was a different person after he stopped drinking.

Ray and Ruth were my father and mother. Their commitment to each other and willingness to strive toward a new home of love and safety healed many wounds. I am the oldest of their four children and Karen is my younger sister. We have all had our own journeys in healing and recovery. Mine included Adult Children of Alcoholics and lots of reading and study. Each of us has a story, but how we made our way through was unique. Our youngest brother's battle was a catalyst for Karen's healing. We are all responsible for our part and decisions on that journey. We come from a background of healing and hope and encourage everyone who reads this book to choose hope.

References

1. Myers, M and Myers, J. (2020). Falling Trees, Color-blind Scientists, and Addiction: A Complete Guide to Addiction for Substance Abusers and Their Families. Ingram Spark.

2. American Psychiatric Association. (2022). Substance-Related and Addictive Disorders. Diagnostic and Statistical Manual of Mental Disorders (5th ed., text rev.), pg. 483-491. https://doi.org/10.1176/appi.books.9780890425787

3. Lipari, R. N. and VanHorn, S. L. (August 24, 2017). "The CBHSQ Report: Children Living with Parents Who Have a Substance Use Disorder." Center for Behavioral Health Statistics and Quality, Substance Abuse and Mental Health Services Adminstration, Rockville, MD. https://www.samhsa.gov/data/sites/default/files/report_3223/ShortReport-3223.html

4. National Center on Substance Abuse and Child Welfare. (2024). Tip Sheet 1 of 3: "Harm Reduction in the Context of Child Well-Being: An Overview for Serving Families Affected by Substance Use Disorders." https://ncsacw.acf.hhs.gov/files/harm-reduction-part1.pdf

5. U.S. Department of Health & Human Services, Administration for Children and Families, Administration on Children, Youth and Families, Children's Bureau. (2024). "Child Maltreatment 2022." Available from https://www.acf.hhs.gov/cb/data-research/child-maltreatment.

6. Augustyn, M., Thornberry, T., Henry, K. (2019, April 16). "The Reproduction of Child Maltreatment: An examination of adolescent problem behavior, substance use, and precocious transitions in the link between victimization and perpetration." https://www.ncbi.nlm.nih.gov/pmc/articles/PMC6467499/

7. Centers for Disease Control and Prevention, National Center for Injury Prevention and Control (2019, November 5). CDC Vital Signs. "Adverse Childhood Events (ACES): Preventing Early Trauma to improve adult health." https://www.cdc.gov/vitalsigns/aces/pdf/vs-1105-aces-H.pdf

8. US Department of Health and Human Services, Administration for Children and Families, Office on Trafficking in Persons. Retrieved April 29, 2024, from https://nhttac.acf.hhs.gov/soar/eguide/stop/adverse_childhood_experiences

9. Trauma Informed Oregon, Regional Research Institute for Human Services, Portland State University. (2024). Adverse Childhood Experiences (ACES): Impact of Childhood Trauma on Adult Well-Being. TIO | Adverse Childhood Experiences (ACE) Study and Trauma (traumainformedoregon.org)

10. Swedo EA, Aslam MV, Dahlberg LL, et al. "Prevalence of Adverse Childhood Experiences Among U.S. Adults — Behavioral Risk Factor Surveillance System, 2011–2020." MMWR Morbidity and Mortality Weekly Report. (2023) 72:707–715. DOI: http://dx.doi.org/10.15585/mmwr.mm7226a2

11. National Scientific Council on the Developing Child (2020). "Connecting the Brain to the Rest of the Body: Early Childhood Development and Lifelong Health Are Deeply Intertwined Working Paper No. 15." Retrieved from https://developingchild.harvard.edu/resources/connecting-the-brain-to-the-rest-of-the-body-early-childhood-development-and-lifelong-health-are-deeply-intertwined/

12. Reviewed by LeWine, H. (2024, April 3). "Understanding the Stress Response: Chronic activation of this survival mechanism impairs health." https://www.health.harvard.edu/staying-healthy/understanding-the-stress-response

13. National Institute on Drug Abuse. (2020, April). "Common Comorbidities with Substance Use Disorders Research Report Part 1: The Connection Between Substance Use Disorders and Mental Illness." https://nida.nih.gov/publications/research-reports/common-comorbidities-substance-use-disorders/part-1-connection-between-substance-use-disorders-mental-illness

14. Hurst, A. (2021, January 4). "43% of Americans—and 56% of Men—Admit to Drinking and Driving." https://www.valuepenguin.com/drinking-habits-survey

15. U.S. Department of Health and Human Services. (2023, January 4). "SAMSHA Announces National Survey on Drug Use and Health (NSDUH) Results Detailing Mental Health and Substance Use Levels in 2021." https://www.hhs.gov/about/news/2023/01/04/samhsa-announces-national-survey-drug-use-health-results-detailing-mental-illness-substance-use-levels-2021.html

16. Cruse, J. and Wegscheider-Cruse, S. (2012). Understanding Codependency, Updated and Expanded: The Science Behing It and How to Break the Cycle. Health Communications Inc. Understanding Codependency, Updated and Expanded | Book by Joseph Cruse, Sharon Wegscheider-Cruse | Official Publisher Page | Simon & Schuster (simonandschuster.com)

17. Prochaska, J and Norcross, J. (2018). Systems of Psychotherapy: A Transtheoretical Analysis. Oxford University Press. https://www.google.com/books/edition/Systems_of_Psychotherapy/4D9FDwAAQBAJ?hl=en

18. Dailey, R. M. (2009). "Confirmation From Family Members: Parent and Sibling Contributions to Adolescent Psychosocial Adjustment." Western Journal of Communication, 73(3), 273–299. https://www.tandfonline.com/doi/abs/10.1080/10570310903082032

19. Neff, K. (2011). Self-Compassion: The Proven Power of Being Kind to Yourself. Harper Collins, New York, NY.

20. U.S. Department of Health and Human Services. (2023, January 4). "SAMSHA Announces National Survey on Drug Use and Health (NSDUH) Results Detailing Mental Health and Substance Use Levels in 2021." https://www.hhs.gov/about/news/2023/01/04/samhsa-announces-national-survey-drug-use-health-results-detailing-mental-illness-substance-use-levels-2021.html

21, 22. National Institute on Drug Abuse. (2020, April). "Common Comorbidities with Substance Use Disorders Research Report Part 1: The Connection Between Substance Use Disorders and Mental Illness." https://nida.nih.gov/publications/research-reports/common-comorbidities-substance-use-disorders/part-1-connection-between-substance-use-disorders-mental-illness

23. McClellan, A.T., Lewis, D.C., O'Brien, C.P., Kleber, HD. (2000, October 4). JAMA – Journal of the American Medical Association. 284:1689-1695. DOI

10.1001/jama.284.13.1689

Index

K

L

M

N

www.ingramcontent.com/pod-product-compliance
Lightning Source LLC
Chambersburg PA
CBHW081143130726
47996CB00009B/2968